Contents

Introduction

I stumbled upon the raw–food diet almost six years ago when I was looking for a way to clear up my skin. It was a discovery that radically changed my life. I didn't have any major health crisis at the time, but I did struggle with acne, arthritis in my hands, headaches, mild depression, and low energy. All of these issues were remedied by switching from a heavy, animal protein–based diet to a juicy plant–based diet of raw fruits and vegetables. I sang raw food's praises everywhere, I bought and read every book out there about this magical diet, and I was in it to win it. My friends and family thought I was crazy, too skinny, rigid, and dogmatic. Thankfully, I've mellowed out over time, shed the dogma, and found balance. I had my ups and downs with the diet and want to share with you my successes as well as my mistakes so that you can go down the raw road smoothly and effortlessly and reap all the benefits it has to offer.

The raw–food movement has evolved during the years that I've been following a mostly raw diet. What was once pushed as an all–or–nothing diet has morphed into less of a niche lifestyle and more of a daily health regimen—kind of like getting your daily exercise, drinking eight glasses of water, or getting enough sleep every night. Now it's "Did I eat enough raw food today?" People are starting to realize that eating fresh, live foods nourishes their bodies, calms cravings, and makes them feel energized. For those who want to take it all the way, eating a 100 percent raw diet is one of the most radically transforming and healing ways to eat. It's something that can be done for as little as a few days to weeks to months to years depending on your health goals. People with cancer, autoimmune diseases, and arthritis have experienced some of the most radical results by eating a simple, clean, raw diet.

I wrote this book to inspire people to eat and live better, not to push my dietary ideals or an extreme diet. In truth, there really aren't that many lifelong, 100 percent raw foodists out there. I have full respect for those who are willing and able to do it, but for the average person, 100 percent raw is not practical, nor is it essential. Everybody has a unique bioindividuality that changes over time, with age, stress, activity level, and seasons. A diet that works for me may not work for you, just as much as a diet that worked wonderfully for you for a while may not serve you down the road. We need to be in tune with what our bodies need and how the food we give them makes us feel. It's all about finding your own personal balance without letting dietary dogma and false promises lead you down the wrong path. No matter where you are on the dietary spectrum—omnivore, paleo/primal, vegetarian, vegan, etc.—everyone can benefit from incorporating raw foods into their diet to whatever degree works for them.

If you're new to raw foods, you have probably picked up a few recipe books that looked a bit intimidating, including my first book, *Going Raw*. Unfamiliar ingredients, lots of soaking, blending, dehydrating, and hours of patience. Forget that. My goal here is to make food fast, fresh, and tasty without having to rearrange your schedule or your kitchen. There's no need for a dehydrator, but if you own one, by all means, use it to warm some of the dishes or dry your nuts and seeds after soaking. I've kept most of the recipes pretty basic, using easy–to–find ingredients, with a few curveballs here and there. Hey, a little variety is good for the soul and the creative juices. I'll show you easy meal planning and what basics to keep on hand at all times so you'll be ready to whip up a great raw meal in a flash.

For those seasoned raw foodists who are looking for new inspiration, I have you in mind as well. Many of us have been misled into thinking we can eat whatever we want as long as it's raw. We've all been on blood–sugar roller coasters and fat–induced comas at some point, and maybe we've eaten more nut butter and Rawtella than we want to admit. There are many gut–busting raw dishes that have left me lethargic instead of energized. I've tried to avoid that in this book. I've kept many of the recipes lighter on the fat content and have experimented with low–glycemic sweeteners. Sugar overload is a big problem in this country, with diabetes rates escalating to new highs. Sugar can be a problem even in its raw–food form, which I address in this book as well. I want everyone to thrive on this diet and feel the best they have ever felt.

Raw–food cuisine has never been easier, more fun, or healthy. I hope you enjoy the journey and find abundant radiance, energy, and vitality along the way.

xoxo,

Judita

CHAPTER ONE 1 WHY RAW ROCKS

After years of eating a high–animal–protein/low–carb diet, I found eating a raw–food diet refreshing and healing. Before switching to raw foods, I felt sluggish and bloated, my skin was a mess, and the diet sodas and coffee I depended on were burning out my adrenals and not supplying me with any real energy. This heavy, acid–forming way of eating was not serving me well, and I knew I had to make a change. Soon after I switched to a raw diet, I lost fifteen pounds (seven kg), my aches and pains went away, and my skin cleared up. Six years later, I still love eating this way. It doesn't mean I don't sometimes eat cooked food, too, but I find whenever I need more pep in my step, sticking to fresh, living foods keeps me energized. The raw diet makes my skin look young and radiant, I can stay up late and wake up early feeling refreshed, and I rarely get sick or suffer from headaches. My story isn't unique in any way. I know people who have dropped more than two hundred pounds, battled cancer, weaned themselves off of insulin, reversed heart disease, and eliminated allergies—all by switching to a raw–food diet. It's not that raw food holds magical powers, it's that our body will heal itself if we let it. Incorporating raw food into your diet gives your body more nutrients and energy to do what it was meant to do.

What Is Raw?

Raw food is food that has not been heated above 118°F (about 48°C) or denatured by chemicals, pasteurization, or irradiation. By keeping food as close to its natural state as possible, we can preserve its nutritional content by up to 70 to 90 percent. Vitamins C and B are especially sensitive to heat degradation, as are the enzymes that help us digest our food more efficiently. Raw preparations such as blending and food processing keep the nutrients intact and allow us to create wonderfully tasty raw dishes.

The major raw food groups are fruits, leafy greens, vegetables, sprouted nuts and seeds, and sea vegetables. The early pioneers of the raw–food health movement were vegans and did not eat animal products, but today some raw foodists include raw dairy, eggs, meat, and fish. I find a plant–based diet is more cleansing and alkalizing, especially if you are switching from a standard American diet (SAD), so I've included only vegetarian recipes in this book. If you choose to eat raw animal products, make sure you get them from a clean and humane source.

Benefits of a Raw–Food Diet

So how exactly does raw food benefit us? Here's an overview of some of the many advantages.

➤ A RAW DIET IS CLEANSING

Our bodies never stop repairing tissue, clearing out toxins, and fighting pathogens, but if we overload our system with processed foods, toxins from cosmetics, toiletries, pesticides, and water and air pollution, our body can't keep up. Toxins build up in our fat tissues, and then our bodies begin to weaken and our health declines. We become susceptible to bacterial and viral infections, our hormones get out of whack, we feel tired and foggy, we have difficulty losing weight, and we are bombarded with free–radical damage that can lead to cancer and accelerated aging. When we eat clean, natural, easy–to–digest food, our bodies have more energy to repair and detoxify and becomes strong and vibrant in every way.

➤ A RAW DIET IS ALKALIZING

Fruits and vegetables contain alkalizing minerals such as calcium, magnesium, and potassium, assists our body in maintaining a proper blood–pH level of 7.35–7.45. When we eat foods that are acidic, our body has to buffer itself by leaching out these minerals from our bones and organs, thereby weakening them. An acidic diet of meat, dairy, wheat, coffee, soda, and alcohol can lead to weight gain, chronic fatigue, osteoporosis, arthritis, and cancer. Ideally we should eat a diet that is 80 percent alkaline and 20 percent acidic foods (I recommend reading *The pH Miracle* by Robert O. Young and Shelley Redford Young for more information on the acid–alkaline balance).

➤ YOU WILL HAVE FEWER CRAVINGS

When we're nutritionally deficient, we can graze on food all day long and never feel satisfied. Eating nutritionally dense foods will calm constant food cravings and make you feel less hungry overall.

➤ YOU WILL HAVE MORE ENERGY

Raw foods don't weigh you down like starchy meals. You'll find you won't need that cup of coffee or afternoon nap after all. No more food comas for you. This is all about eating for energy!

➤ YOUR HORMONES WILL BE MORE IN BALANCE

Diet and lifestyle have a profound effect on hormonal balance. Many women have experienced less breast tenderness, water retention, and cramping, and fewer breakouts and hot flashes, after switching to a low–sugar, raw–food diet.

➤ YOU WILL BE BETTER HYDRATED

Most people don't drink enough water and are chronically dehydrated. Raw foods have more water content than cooked foods, which helps our kidneys function better, makes our skin look supple, and gives us more energy and better mental focus.

➤ YOU WILL HAVE BETTER DIGESTION

The high fiber and water content in raw foods helps keep things moving along in the intestinal tract, sweeping out old matter and toxins. You'll be more regular, have a flatter tummy, and feel less sluggish and bloated.

➤ YOUR IMMUNE SYSTEM WILL BE STRONGER

Raw food has high amounts of vitamin C and phytonutrients, which have strong immune–enhancing, antioxidant, anti–inflammatory, and anti–cancer properties. They also protect our cardiovascular system and prevent macular degeneration and osteoporosis.

➤ A RAW DIET CONTAINS CHLOROPHYLL

All green vegetables contain chlorophyll, also known as plant blood (think wheatgrass shots). This substance is highly alkalizing, contains anti–carcinogenic properties, builds up our red blood cells, oxygenates the blood, and chelates toxic heavy metals such as mercury. Cooking quickly degrades this powerful compound.

➤ YOU WILL LOSE WEIGHT

It's inevitable that a low–calorie, fiber–rich raw diet will help you shed the extra weight. Adding more raw food and crowding out junky processed food will help you slim down fast!

➤ A RAW DIET SLOWS DOWN THE AGING PROCESS

Flooding our body with nutrients every day keeps our organs functioning properly, giving us better energy, mental clarity, and hormonal balance—and fewer wrinkles. Your risk of getting age–related diseases also decreases. No more worrying about heart disease, high blood pressure, or high cholesterol.

Essential Nutrients

It is, indeed, possible to meet your recommended dietary allowance (RDA) of vitamins and minerals by eating a raw vegan diet. The key is eating a variety of foods, especially greens. Here is a list of some of the essential nutrients and where to find them.

➤ PROTEIN

In the United States, we are obsessed with protein. We eat much more of it than people do in any other country—often more than our bodies need. The average adult woman needs 46 grams of protein per day, while an adult male needs around 56 grams. The good news is, you can get your protein fix from plants, as all contain some amount of protein. Protein is made up of amino acids that are essential for repairing tissue, forming cells, and making antibodies, and are an integral part of enzyme and hormonal activity. If you're pregnant or an athlete, you'll need to bump up your intake, but for the average person, meeting your daily needs is fairly easy.

The best sources are:
- Green leafy vegetables, especially kale and spinach
- Sprouts
- Almonds
- Pumpkin seeds
- Hemp seeds
- Chia seeds
- Flax seeds
- Sunflower seeds
- Goji berries
- Cacao nibs
- Buckwheat
- Oats

Health Note: If you're a "protein type" and don't feel satisfied on a raw diet, try adding a raw vegan protein powder, such as Sun Warrior, to your smoothies. In the afternoon, when I feel my energy dip, I blend a scoop of vanilla or chocolate protein power with a cup of almond milk and I perk right up. Way better than coffee—and without any side effects.

➤ CALCIUM

To build strong bones, you need more than just calcium. You need vitamin D to assimilate the calcium, and you also need bone–building minerals like silica and magnesium. You can find calcium in:
- Sesame seeds (tahini)
- Kale
- Collards
- Broccoli
- Bok choy
- Endive
- Kelp
- Figs

➤ VITAMIN D

Spend ten to fifteen minutes in the sun every day or take a vitamin D_2 (ergocalciferol) or D_3 (cholecalciferol) supplement. D_2 comes from a plant source, whereas D_3 comes from animal sources. The latter is more bioavailable, but both are effective.

➤ SILICA AND MAGNESIUM

These bone–building minerals are also great for the skin and heart.

Find them in these delicious sources:
- Pumpkin seeds
- Spinach
- Apples
- Oranges
- Cherries
- Cucumber
- Onions
- Beets
- Celery
- Almonds
- Cacao
- Bananas
- Figs
- Horsetail (tea)
- Nettle (tea)

➤ IRON

Iron carries oxygen through the blood and helps build red blood cells. It absorbs better when vitamin C is present. An easy way to combine them is to eat sources of iron with lemon juice or tomatoes in a salad.

The best sources are:
- Pumpkin seeds
- Sesame seeds
- Sunflower seeds
- Kale
- Romaine lettuce
- Kelp
- Broccoli
- Bok choy

➤ ESSENTIAL FATTY ACIDS

Omega–6 is abundant in any diet; it's the omega–3s we really need to focus on. Omega–3s reduce inflammation and pain, improve brain function, and reduce the risk of heart disease and stroke.

The best sources are:
- Flaxseeds and flaxseed oil
- Chia seeds and chia seed oil
- Hemp seeds and hemp seed oil
- Green leafy vegetables
- Sacha inchi seeds and sacha inchi oil
- Sea vegetables
- Walnuts
- Broccoli

➤ VITAMIN B$_{12}$

A B$_{12}$ deficiency is a major health problem that can leave you with depression, agitation, memory loss, muscle fatigue, and permanent nerve and neurological damage. This is one area where a raw vegan diet falls short, as there are no adequate plant sources of natural B$_{12}$. But studies show that even meat–eaters can be deficient. The best way to guarantee you're getting enough of it is by using a transdermal patch or a sublingual tablet of methylcobalamin. I stick a transdermal patch behind my ear twice a week and my B$_{12}$ levels are perfect.

Cooking up a Storm of Health Problems

One of the major benefits of going raw isn't just what you're eating, but what you're *not* eating. Eliminating processed foods that contain trans fats, refined sugars, artificial flavors and coloring, and preservatives is a huge step toward better wellness. Cooking can create a host of carcinogenic substances, too, like acrylamides, advanced glycation end–products (AGEs), heterocyclic amines, and polycyclic aromatic hydrocarbons. These are the result of heating oils, animal proteins, starches, and sugars. They have been shown to impair the immune system, alter DNA, accelerate aging, increase inflammation, and increase cancer risk.

Eliminating other substances such as coffee and alcohol can make a big difference in your health, as well. Coffee is dehydrating, creates hormonal imbalance, blocks iron absorption, stresses the body, and gives you a false sense of energy. Alcohol is also dehydrating, weakens your bones, and causes depression, weight gain, and hormonal imbalance. I'm not saying you can't ever enjoy these again, but they're not a regular part of a truly healthy lifestyle.

Making It Work for You

No diet is one size fits all. We are all unique and have different needs, heath issues, and goals, so I never advocate to my clients an all–or–nothing approach to raw foods. Everyone needs to find their own path and not compare themselves to others. Raw is not a religion, it's a tool—one of many—that can help you reach great health. I do believe that aiming for 50 percent raw is ideal for many people and can be done simply by adding a smoothie for breakfast and a salad for lunch or dinner. In fact, just eating one raw meal a day, such as a smoothie for breakfast, can make significant changes. Victoria Boutenko, raw food expert and author of *Green For Life*, challenged twenty–seven people to drink one quart (two pints) of green smoothie for breakfast for one month in addition to their regular diet. Twenty–four participants reported positive changes, which included increased energy, better digestion,

less blood sugar fluctuation, better sleep, clearer skin, stronger fingernails, less dandruff, and better sex. What have you got to lose except poor health?

Once you reach 50 percent raw, try 75 percent. Then try 100 percent and see how you feel. For newbies, going 100 percent overnight can be a bit of a shock for the body. Even at 75 percent raw, you can expect detox symptoms such as headaches, junk–food cravings, mood swings, fatigue, and gas. I always recommend starting slow and gradually working your way up to where you're comfortable. As you add more raw, start letting go of processed foods, fried foods, caffeine, meat, dairy, wheat, and other glutinous foods. Go one step at a time and watch your health completely transform.

Raw Transitional Plan

The following is a guideline for people who would like to try a high–raw meal plan. It is by no means the only way to go raw. You may prefer to take a different route, such as eating a cooked meal for breakfast and going raw for dinner. It's totally up to you to design a meal plan that is right for you. A high raw diet may or may not be right, so listen to your body, go with the flow, and customize this to work for you.

➤ FIRST WEEK: 50% RAW

Morning: Raw breakfast
Lunch: Raw side salad + your regular lunch
Raw snack
Dinner: Raw side salad + your regular dinner
Raw dessert (if desired)

➤ SECOND WEEK: 75% RAW

Morning: Raw breakfast
Lunch: Raw lunch
Raw snack
Dinner: Raw side salad + your regular dinner
Raw dessert (if desired)

➤ THIRD WEEK: 100% RAW

Morning: Raw breakfast
Lunch: Raw lunch
Raw snack
Dinner: Raw dinner
Raw dessert (if desired)

Building a Lifetime of Great Health

The raw food lifestyle isn't just about food. It's about creating the best health possible through cleansing, exercise, sleep, and other healthy habits. Here are some of my best health strategies that I follow and teach to my clients.

➤ GET A WATER FILTER

"Get a filter or be a filter," I've heard raw food expert and speaker David Wolfe say. The Environmental Working Group (EWG) has found 315 pollutants—including chlorine, fluoride, arsenic, radon, radiation, mercury, and chromium–6—in American tap water. Since it takes a long time for these toxins to accumulate in the body, there has never been any solid evidence connecting tap water to a particular illness, but any logical person could agree the less exposure we have to these substances, the better health we'll have. A whole–house water filtration system is ideal, but expensive. At the very least have a filter in the shower and the kitchen for drinking, cleaning, and preparing food.

➤ REPLACE YOUR COSMETICS, LOTIONS, AND POTIONS

Toss out toxic makeup, hair products, moisturizers, and nail polish. There are many companies making good–quality products free of toxins and carcinogens that age us and steal our beauty. The EWG has rated more than 74,000 beauty products based on their toxicity. Check out their Skin Deep Cosmetic Database (www.ewg.org/skindeep) to see where your favorite products stack up.

➤ GO GREEN WITH HOUSECLEANERS

Don't clean your house or clothing with bleach or other caustic chemicals. There are many products that do the same job and make your house and clothes smell pleasant, not antiseptic. Laundry detergents and fabric softeners contain xenoestrogens that can lead to hormonal imbalance. Since we wear clothes all day and sleep on bedding at night, we are constantly absorbing these xenoestrogens. Instead use Nature Clean powder detergent and distilled vinegar in the rinse cycle as a fabric softener.

➤ GROW YOUR OWN FRESH AIR

Air inside our homes can become more toxic than air in the outside world as off–gassing from furniture, kitchen cabinets, flooring, carpeting, and paint pollute our living spaces. Keep your windows open as much as possible and place houseplants in every room to filter the air. A wonderful book called *How to Grow Your Own Fresh Air* by B. C. Wolverton is a great guide to purifying your environment with plants.

➤ EAT REAL FOOD

Avoid processed, prepackaged foods. They're loaded with preservatives, artificial ingredients, hydrogenated fats, MSG, genetically modified ingredients, and sodium. Avoid pesticides by eating organic foods.

Removing Toxins from Our Body

The average person has about three hundred to five hundred industrial chemicals, pesticides, and pollutants in his or her bloodstream. Scientists have even tested umbilical cords from newborn babies and found the presence of two hundred industrial toxins. That's a lot of chemicals to have in your system the day you're born! In this modern age, we really have to make a lifelong effort to minimize additional exposure to toxins and actively do things to move them out of our body. There are many great books out there on detoxification, but here are a few things you can do right away to move them out of your system quickly.

➤ SWEAT IT OUT

Our skin is a major detoxifying organ. Whenever we sweat we push out toxins from our fat tissues. We can sweat it out at the gym or in a sauna. Far infrared sauna is one of the best methods because the far infrared waves penetrate 1½ inches (3.8 cm) into our skin, which helps draw out the toxins. It operates at a lower temperature than hot rock saunas so you can stay in this sauna for much longer.

➤ REBOUNDING

Also known as the mini trampoline, rebounding is a fun way to get the lymphatic system moving while burning calories. The up and down movement helps stimulate white blood cells while lymph sweeps away bacteria, viruses, and toxins. Two minutes of rebounding several times a day will help strengthen your immune system, as well as your bones and every cell in your body. If you don't have a rebounder, jumping rope works, too!

➤ CLEANSE YOUR COLON

A sluggish colon is a toxic colon. If you're not going to the bathroom two to three times a day, you are holding toxins in your colon that can re-enter the bloodstream and damage your cells. It's basically self-poisoning. In fact, the average adult walks around with ten pounds of waste in their gut from constipation, making them bloated, headachy, and tired. We can easily move it out with what is known as the oldest medical procedure in history: colon cleansing. Professional colon hydrotherapy is about the equivalent of four to six bowel movements in one session. It cleans out waste, parasites, yeast, and old debris while helping to hydrate and strengthen the colon to improve digestion. If you prefer some alone time, another option is home enemas. Enema bags are very affordable, and there are many websites that can explain how to use them correctly. I recommend getting a four-quart bag, which is almost as efficient as a professional colonic. You can add probiotics, lemon juice, apple cider vinegar, wheatgrass, or even lukewarm organic coffee, which is extremely detoxifying for the liver. A coffee enema, if done properly, will not affect you the same way as drinking it will. Don't knock it till you try it. Many people report major improvement in skin conditions, backaches, headaches, and chronic fatigue after colon cleansing.

➤ DRY SKIN BRUSHING

Gliding a dry, coarse, natural bristle brush on your skin before showering aids the lymphatic system while improving circulation and removing dead skin cells so your skin can detoxify more efficiently. Brushing your skin is very enjoyable and takes only two minutes a day to complete. Start at your hands and feet and brush toward your heart. The bristles may seem scratchy at first, but soon you will grow to love it. Do this daily and watch your skin texture and cellulite improve in thirty days.

➤ TAKE SUPPLEMENTS

There are hundreds of products and herbs that can aid the detoxification process. Here are some of the all-stars:

- **Chlorella** purifies the blood and is very good at removing toxins from the intestines, including heavy metals, pesticides, and radiation particles from cancer therapy. With the amount of radiation that presently is in our environment, this is a great supplement to be taking daily for protection.
- **Zeolite** is created when volcanic ash and lava comes in contact with alkaline ground water. It's ground into a fine powder and used in many natural detergents. Its negative charge attracts and traps toxins and heavy metals, making it an excellent detoxifier.
- **Burdock root** also known as gobo, is popular in Asian cuisine. It's a very powerful liver and blood cleanser, inhibits bacteria and molds, stimulates skin circulation and detoxification, and helps support kidney function. It can be juiced or chopped and steeped in boiling water to make a tea. It can be very helpful with arthritis and skin conditions.
- **Dandelion root and leaves** are great for supporting the liver, gallbladder, and kidneys. It's a diuretic and increases the flow of bile and gastric juices, purifies the blood, and tones the digestive tract. Drink dandelion root tea and eat the green leaves in a salad or in a juice or green smoothie.
- **MSM, or methyl-sulfonyl-methane**, is a sulfur compound that can be acquired by eating foods that contain sulfur. It's very good at removing mercury as well as old accumulated toxins. It's also quite powerful and should be taken at very small doses at first: ⅛ of a teaspoon a day for starters, and then up to 1–2 tablespoons (28–55 g) per day, but only if you have no side effects. Look for plant-derived MSM from wood pulp only.

➤ EXERCISE

Exercise is an integral part of a healthy lifestyle—not only does it strengthen our bones and muscles, but it also increases circulation to help accelerate the release of toxins and accumulated waste. If you're doing a detox that includes fasting, then you don't want to do anything too strenuous, but you do want to keep moving. In addition to the rebounding I mentioned earlier, gentle exercises like yoga and qigong are two ways to exercise while stimulating the body to release toxins and balance itself.

Juice Fasting

Fasting is a great way to deeply detoxify, reboot your system, and shed some extra weight. When your body doesn't have to digest food, it has more energy to clean out toxins and fight pathogens. While fasting, you'll find yourself alternating between unbounded energy and laser mental focus—and then headaches, fatigue, and intense cravings. This is normal as you go through processed–food withdrawals and release old, stored toxins from your fat tissue. The first three days are the most challenging, which is why weekends at home are the ideal way to kick off a fast. After that it's smooth sailing.

➤ THE PLAN

I recommend only one to five days for beginners, and six to fourteen days for the more experienced. Any longer than that is best done with a fasting expert or health coach. If you want to go it alone, check out *Raw Food Cleanse* by Penni Shelton for juicing plans and additional recipes. If you like a little support, try finding some fasting companions online. If you live in the United States, for instance, you can cleanse with hundreds of other people across the country at www.cleanseamerica.com.

The best time of year to fast is during the changing of the seasons, particularly spring and fall, when it's warm and fresh produce is abundant. I recommend getting extra rest during this time, but you may do light exercise such as rebounding, walking, or casual bicycling. I'd avoid anything strenuous or vigorous.

Here's what to do:

- Drink 3–4 quarts (12–16 cups) or more of fresh juice a day. At least half should be vegetable juices. Pace yourself and have 1 quart (4 cups) each at breakfast, lunch, mid–afternoon, and dinner.
- If you're on a candida cleanse or have blood sugar issues, you should avoid all fruit juices except for ones containing green apples, lemons, or limes, which are low sugar.
- Chew your juice. Swish green juice around your teeth to help mineralize them and chew to activate your digestive system. This will help the body absorb and utilize the nutrients more efficiently.
- I like to drink 8–16 ounces of fresh almond or cashew milk (page 59), as well, when I'm fasting. The small amount of fat really takes the edge off, especially in the first three days. Flavor it with vanilla and your favorite sweetener, if you'd like.

To keep things moving along the intestinal tract, I recommend an herbal digestive stimulator. Healthforce Nutritionals makes a great one that is gentle and noncramping. Having a colon hydrotherapy session before and after a fast or doing daily home enemas is highly recommended. The colon can become very toxic if constipation arises and those toxins can be reintroduced into your bloodstream, making you feel ill and tired.

➤ ENDING A FAST

Always reintroduce solid foods slowly when breaking a fast. Your metabolism slows when you fast, so eating a high–calorie meal right out of the gate will cause those calories to go straight into fat storage instead of being used for fuel because your body doesn't know you've been fasting. Your body's survival mechanism thinks there's a food shortage and that food may continue to be scarce in the future, so it conserves fat stores. (Note: That's the reason why crash diets never work!) Also, our stomach's ability to produce hydrochloric acid (HCl) declines during fasting and needs to be reignited. Without HCl we have difficulty breaking down, digesting, and absorbing our food. If you don't slowly reintroduce food to your diet, you will run the risk of rapid weight gain and major digestive distress. You've been warned!

Divide the number of days you fasted in half to determine the number of days you should take to return to your regular diet. For example, if you fasted for six days, then you will take three days to ease back into your regular eating habits.

Break your fast with a mono meal of raw fruit. This is where you only eat one kind of fruit in a sitting, such as a bowl of grapes or sliced tomatoes for the low–sugar crowd. This is going to taste like one of the best meals of your life. Don't forget to chew it well!

For the rest of the day have a simple fruit or vegetable smoothie. The next day have simple salads with some avocado along with more smoothies. You can have denser meals the following day but be mindful of portion sizes until your digestive fire returns and your metabolism is back to normal.

Last but not least, please make sure you contact your physician before embarking on a fast if you have any medical health issues.

Hot Tip! Many juice bars and companies have popped up recently that offer three– to five–day juice packages. This can save you a lot of time and be a great option if you don't own a juicer.

Smoothie Fasting

For some people, juice fasting is a little too radical. If that's you, I suggest trying a smoothie fast. Like juices, smoothies put very little strain on the digestive system, and you'll have less hunger, constipation, and other juicing side effects. This method doesn't produce as deep of a cleanse, but it's a great option for people who are hypoglycemic, don't need intense cleansing, don't want to disrupt their normal lives, or don't own a juicer. Your metabolism won't slow down like it would during a juice fast, and you can resume eating normally when you're done. Another plus is that it's much quicker to blend a smoothie than it is to juice 4 quarts (16 cups) of fruits and vegetables. It's also less expensive, as you would need four times as many vegetables to create the same amount of juice.

➤ THE PLAN

- You can do this for as little as one day or as long as you like. I enjoy one to two days when I've overindulged and need to lighten up and give my digestion a break. If I want to thin out a bit, I'll go five to seven days.
- Drink 3–4 quarts (12–16 cups) of fruit and vegetable smoothies a day–one each at breakfast, lunch, midafternoon, and dinner.

- If you are sugar sensitive or on a candida–elimination diet, make your smoothies low glycemic by choosing low–sugar fruits like strawberries, or make vegetable smoothies or soups. You can use any of the smoothies in this book as well as the smooth soups such as Carrot–Ginger Coconut (page 77), Curried Cauliflower (page 81), and Cucumber Basil (page 74).
- If you want to lose weight, use avocado and coconut in moderation. Reducing fat will also give your liver and gallbladder a rest. If you want to maintain your weight, make sure to include the fats.
- Keep salt to a minimum, but if you can go salt free, even better. You'll lose water weight and reawaken your taste buds. Breaking free of salt dependence is much healthier, especially if you are suffering from hypertension.
- You can use chia seeds to thicken your smoothies and add some extra fiber and sustenance.

If you're interested in a guided smoothie detox program, I highly recommend Dr. Ritamarie Loscalzo's online Green Cleanse Program (www.drritamarie.com/greencleanse#).

Raw for Weight Loss

People go raw for many different reasons, but most of the clients who come to me want to lose extra weight. Here are my best tips on how to lose weight with raw foods.

➤ EAT A LOW–SUGAR RAW DIET

Avoid highly sweet fruits such as tropical fruits and keep dates and agave to a minimum. Also skip oats and grains.

➤ DON'T EAT PAST 6 P.M.

Nighttime eating slows digestion, and anything still in the stomach when you go to bed will get stored as fat. Inversely, if you are afraid of losing too much weight on raw (guys, I'm talking to you), eat later in the day, but not so much that you can't sleep well.

➤ SLEEP

If you don't get enough sleep, you won't produce the hormones that help you burn fat. Lack of sleep also affects the hunger hormone leptin. Leptin signals our brain that we are not hungry. Get at least seven to eight hours of sleep a night.

➤ DO MINI FASTS

Eat a light dinner like Cucumber Basil Soup (page 74), then skip breakfast and hit the gym in the morning. Break your fast with a sensible lunch like Chipotle Wraps (page 124). Avoid any fructose or sugars until at least two hours after your workout. Do this once or twice a week. It's a great way to overcome plateaus in your diet. Doing mini fasts can help you increase your Human Growth Hormone by 1,300–2,000 percent!

➤ DO A SEVEN–DAY JUICE OR SMOOTHIE FAST

Toxins in the body can prevent you from releasing excess weight. A smoothie or juice fast can flush those toxins out.

If you've tried everything and you're still struggling to lose weight, see your doctor about having your hormone levels checked. You could be dealing with thyroid or other endocrine issues. Estrogen dominance makes it very difficult to lose weight and can be remedied by following a xenoestrogen elimination diet (page 18).

Human Growth Hormone

Growth hormone, also known as human growth hormone (HGH), is an anabolic hormone secreted by the pituitary gland. It is essential to helping us grow when we're adolescents, but it is also a major fat–burning hormone that builds muscle, improves brain function and memory, and strengthens bones, among many other actions. We produce large amounts of it when we are young and less of it as we age. Celebrities and bodybuilders inject dangerous synthetic HGH to keep their youthful appearance and muscularity, but we can up our bodies' own production of HGH very easily through sleep, exercise, and diet.

1. SLEEP

Studies have shown that there is a circadian rhythm to our hormonal surges throughout the day. We release HGH in surges every three to five hours, and the largest amount of HGH is released when we sleep, so make it a priority to get at least seven to eight hours of uninterrupted sleep per night. The biggest HGH surge happens sixty to ninety minutes after we fall asleep and most abundantly around midnight, so if you regularly burn the midnight oil, you might want to consider hitting the hay by 10 p.m. or 11 p.m.

2. EXERCISE

Depending on your preference, there are two ways of exercising that are very efficient at stimulating HGH:

Interval cardio training.
This where you do short bursts of intense aerobic activity for thirty seconds at a time. My preferred method is on a stationary bike. I warm up for two to three minutes at an easy pace then do a thirty–second burst as fast as I can, then return to my easy pace. Once my heart rate returns to normal, I do another burst. You can also do this when walking. Just increase your pace during the burst to a brisk walk or a full run, depending on your fitness level. Four to eight bursts per session, once or twice a week is sufficient.

Resistance strength training
Engaging your muscles using weights and kettle bells also helps stimulate growth hormone. Schedule a personal training session at your gym to learn how to strength train properly. Two times a week will do, as overtraining causes inflammation and releases cortisol.

3. DIET

The presence of insulin turns off the release of HGH, so eating a low–glycemic diet is essential.

Don't eat anything sugary, including fruit, or starches like pasta or rice before exercising or two hours after your workout. A great post–workout meal would be an unsweetened Cashew Hemp Milk (page 59) protein shake and a green salad like Creamy Kale Salad (page 106).

Eating sweets or starches before bed will shut off your nightly HGH release. Make sure you eat your last meal at least three hours before you go to bed. If you're going to have a big meal, have it four to five hours before bed.

Don't graze. You will release more HGH if you avoid eating between meals. Eat enough to keep you full for four to five hours and skip the snacking.

Stress also prevents the release of growth hormone and increases fat–storing cortisol. Live a life of balance so daily stress doesn't sabotage your diet and happiness.

Xenoestrogens

Xenoestrogens are foreign chemical compounds that mimic estrogen, the female hormone, in the body. Both men and women are becoming very estrogenic from exposure to chemicals like Bisphenol A (BPA), which is found in plastic water bottles, can and juice box liners, and store receipts. Other sources of xenoestrogens come from fuel and fuel exhaust, plastic products and cookware, Teflon–coated pans, Styrofoam, pesticides, insecticides, and hundreds of different solvents, paints, personal beauty and hygiene products, and commercially raised meat and dairy that has been injected with recombinant bovine growth hormone, or rBGH.

Excess estrogen, also called estrogen dominance, has been linked to breast cancer, fibroids, endometriosis, cysts, and early puberty in girls. In men it can cause prostate cancer, gynecomastia ("man boobs"), and delayed puberty in boys.

➤ TO REDUCE YOUR XENOESTROGEN EXPOSURE:

Avoid plastic bottles and storage containers. Use BPA–free water bottles and glass containers instead.

Don't use conventional detergents or fabric softeners. I recommend Nature Clean powdered detergent over any others, including eco detergent brands.

Buy organic everything.

Avoid parabens, phthalates, and phenoxyethanol, which are often used in lotions, baby powder, and shampoos.

Avoid exposure to industrial chemicals such as paint, varnish, bleach, solvents, even nail polish and removers. Sorry, ladies: Don't go to nail salons unless they're eco–friendly, or bring your own nontoxic polish and remover.

Remove excess estrogens by eating cruciferous vegetables such as cabbage, kale, broccoli, and bok choy. They contain a phytochemical called indole–3–carbinol, a compound that removes these bad estrogens and restores hormonal balance. You can find indole–3–carbinol supplements at most health food stores, but don't use them in place of eating veggies. Following many of the detoxing methods outlined on page 14 such as sweating and using liver herbs, will help move the bad estrogen out, too.

Understanding Your Cravings

The most common complaint I hear from people coming from a SAD diet is that they can't seem to control their cravings. It sabotages their ability to stick to a healthy diet, and they feel helpless and out of control. I've been there and I know it's hard—I had a Diet Coke addiction for more than twenty years. Simply put, cravings are just messages from your body. They're not bad per se, they're just signals from our body that it needs something. Cravings can be put into two categories: physiological and emotional.

Physiological cravings can stem from mineral deficiency, chemical addiction, dehydration, or lack of energy.

➤ MINERAL DEFICIENCY

If we're not eating a balanced diet, we may be lacking the essential nutrients our body needs. Start your day with a mineral-rich green juice or green smoothie. Powdered green whole-food supplements are also great. When your body has all the nutrients it needs, it won't be constantly hungry.

➤ FOOD CHEMICAL ADDICTIONS

Processed foods are created in such a way that you will crave them again and again. This is by design. If you have a food that you say you can't live without, then it has an ingredient that is creating an opiate effect that you are addicted to. Even whole foods like cheese and wheat contain proteins that stimulate dopamine production. In processed foods it's a bit more sinister, as MSG, high-fructose corn syrup, and aspartame are not only addictive, but also harmful to the body. The best way to rid yourself of food chemical cravings is to go cold turkey with these junk-food chemicals and let your taste buds discover new and exciting foods.

➤ LACK OF ENERGY

One of the most common reasons we have cravings is because we are looking for energy. We often reach for sugar when we feel like we're lagging; our body knows this is the fastest way to get energy. If it's a late-night craving, I recommend just turning in. If it's the mid-afternoon slump, I recommend a little nap if you can swing it. Otherwise, drink a green juice or a protein shake. Green juice will oxygenate the blood and perk you up physically, while the amino acids will give you a mental boost.

➤ DEHYDRATION

We can often mistake dehydration for hunger. Whenever you get any kind of craving, always drink a tall glass of water first and wait a few minutes to see if you're still hungry.

➤ LOW LEPTIN PRODUCTION

Leptin is known as the hunger hormone. Formed in our fat cells, it signals the brain when we have had enough to eat. It also increases our appetite when our fat (energy) reserves are low and reduces hunger when we have extra energy reserves. Have you ever had a big meal and an hour later felt like you were starving again? This means your leptin level is too low or you may be leptin resistant, which is when a high level of leptin circulates in the bloodstream but the body is immune to it. It's very similar to insulin resistance, which is when the cells are no longer receptive to insulin. We can increase our leptin production and sensitivity to it naturally by not eating after dinner, getting enough sleep every night, and eating a low–glycemic, fiber–rich, non–inflammatory diet high in omega–3 fatty acids.

➤ CANDIDA OVERGROWTH

Candida thrives on sugar. As it proliferates throughout our body, its demand for sugar rises and cravings can become fierce. Eating probiotic–rich foods like sauerkraut and coconut kefir can eliminate sugar cravings within days.

➤ DIRTY MOUTH

Food left in our mouths after eating can stimulate cravings. If you can't brush, chew some xylitol dental gum after meals.

Emotional cravings can come from stress, boredom, lack of joy, and emotional pain.

➤ STRESS

Stress causes cortisol levels to rise, which creates intense food cravings and binging. Manage stress and lower cortisol by exercising regularly, going for walks, meditating, deep breathing, or talking it out with a friend or loved one.

➤ BOREDOM

Boredom can lead to cravings as well. If you're eating because you're bored, do an activity that you love. Remember when you were a kid and you were too busy playing to stop and eat? Find things that you love to do and get lost in them.

➤ EMOTIONAL PAIN

Emotional pain can lead to eating because we are lacking joy in our lives or numbing a painful feeling. This is only temporary and does nothing to fix a difficult situation. Dissatisfaction with a relationship, feeling unfulfilled in a career, lacking a sense of spiritual purpose—all of this and more can drive us to consume comfort foods, but only by taking action in those areas can we get to the root of emotional eating. A good health coach can help you navigate and master your food cravings if you feel you need more support in this area.

➤ ONE FINAL NOTE ON MASTERING YOUR CRAVINGS

Eliminate all junk foods from your kitchen as well as "trigger" foods—foods that cause you to binge when you said you were only going to have just one. If there is a food that turns you into Cookie Monster, then that food is no longer allowed in the house. This includes raw foods like raw cookies and cakes.

Mindful Eating

Many of us don't stop to appreciate the food we put into our bodies. We live in a fast–food, convenience–dependent society, where we mindlessly eat in our cars and in front of the television or computer. I used to be one of those people. If we can slow down and start to pay attention to what we're doing, savor the flavors and textures of our food, and enjoy company or quiet solitude during our meals, we can reduce overeating and improve digestion and assimilation of nutrients.

My tips for having the best meal ever:

➤ PREPARE FOOD WITH POSITIVE INTENTION AND LOVE

There is something to putting good vibrations into what we think, say, and create. Whenever I make food for my family and friends I always add vitamin Love to it. It may seem a bit hippy for some, but there is anecdotal evidence showing that saying a small prayer over food can bring healing, joy, and empowerment for those who eat it. There's certainly no harm in doing it, and it will give you a moment to reflect on those who are important to you.

➤ DON'T EAT WHEN YOU'RE IN A BAD MOOD

Have you ever lost your appetite when someone told you bad news? Have you ever had to run to the bathroom because you were so nervous? Do you get butterflies when you meet a cute guy/girl? Our gut is actually our second brain. It contains a vast network of neurons and neurotransmitters and is connected via major nerves to our brain. When one gets upset, so does the other. If you're emotionally upset, your stomach "goes into knots"

and stops digesting. This is the worst time to try to eat, as you will get major indigestion and your body won't be able to properly assimilate the nutrients. Eating when we're stressed, sad, or upset in order to numb our emotions is also a bad habit many people fall into. Emotional eating leads to overeating and binging, which leads to feelings of guilt as we scold ourselves for lacking self–control. If you're upset, go for a walk and get some fresh air and sun or go to a quiet room and do some deep breathing and meditation. Once you feel balanced and calm, enjoy your meal.

➤ CHEW YOUR FOOD BEFORE SWALLOWING

I admit I was the worst at chewing my food, but once I mastered the art of slowing down I had much better digestion. The secret is take a bite, put your fork down, and chew, chew, chew. Your stomach doesn't have teeth, so it's up to you to make food as easy as possible to digest as it makes it journey down the digestive tract. You don't have to count to thirty with each bite. Just make sure what you're swallowing is completely liquid. By taking the extra time to eat, my stomach was able to tell my brain it was full before I had time to run to get a second helping.

➤ DON'T READ OR WATCH TV WHILE YOU EAT

This mindless eating is what makes us overeat the most. We're too distracted to realize we're not hungry any more. In addition, we're not paying attention to how good (or bad) the food is. Ideally, eat without distraction. Look at your food, smell it, and savor the flavors one bite at a time.

10 Raw and Simple Lifestyle Tips

Optimal health isn't just about the food we eat. Simple daily practices can make the quality of our life the best ever.

1. DRINK WATER

   Drink six to eight glasses a day of clean, filtered water. Start the day by drinking two cups of those soon as you wake up. Doing so helps curb false hunger, gives you energy, and flushes your kidneys.

2. EXERCISE EVERY DAY

   Do some kind of exercise for at least twenty minutes a day. Walk, jog, cycle, stretch, rebound—whatever. Just move. Exercise oxygenates the body, gets the lymphatic system going, and helps clear the mind. I come up with my best ideas when I'm exercising.

3. GET FRESH AIR

   Keep the windows in your home open to circulate stagnant, polluted indoor air. Even in the dead of winter, it's good to open your windows and freshen the air for a few minutes.

4. SLEEP

   At the very minimum, get seven hours of shut-eye a night. Don't keep your cell phone near your head. Turn it off or set it to airplane mode so you're not bombarded with electromagnetic fields, or EMFs, while you sleep. Researchers have found radiofrequency radiation from cell phones negatively affect brain activity even when the phones are not in use. Unplug lamps and clocks as well. Make your bedroom a sanctuary free from every environmental pollutant so you can wake up rested and ready to rock and roll.

5. MANAGE STRESS

   Meditate, pray, go for walks, talk it out. Do whatever you have to do to get balanced. Stress is considered the number one silent killer in America. The overproduction of cortisol exhausts our adrenals, puts on belly fat, throws off our hormones, and ages us. Stress has been linked to heart disease, insomnia, digestive disorders, depression, and obesity.

6. SOAK UP THE SUNSHINE

   The sun isn't something to be afraid of. Spend ten to fifteen minutes a day in the sun without sunscreen to activate the synthesis of vitamin D. Vitamin D gives us strong bones and strong immune function. The sun's healing light is great for acne and for lifting your mood. It increases production

of serotonin and melatonin, helping to regulate our sleep patterns and prevent seasonal affective disorder.

7. GET GROUNDED

   Walk barefoot in the yard or in a park and get reconnected to the earth. There is much evidence to show that touching the earth discharges the electromagnetic radiation that we are exposed to through cellphone, radio, and TV towers, and through the EMF in our homes like electrical wiring, computers, and appliances. As EMF exposure builds up in your body, you can feel fatigue, anxiety, nervousness, and stress. You can buy grounding bed sheets and gadgets for the home, but it costs nothing to go barefoot in the grass (or even concrete) for a few minutes every day. After every flight I always take off my shoes and touch the earth for several minutes to help reset my circadian rhythm and release negative energy. Try it next time you travel and see how much quicker you recover from jetlag.

8. VALIDATE THE IMPORTANT PEOPLE IN YOUR LIFE

   Tell them you love and appreciate them and that they matter. The day before I unexpectedly lost my mother I had meant to call her, but I procrastinated. The next day she was gone. Do it for yourself and for them. How great is to hear from someone that you're important in his or her life? Spread the love.

9. HOLD NO GRUDGES

   Don't carry anger with you. It creates stress, releases cortisol levels, interferes with sleep, and exhausts you mentally and emotionally. If someone has done you wrong, forgive him or her—even if the person doesn't ask for it. Life is too short to spend it thinking about other people's actions. Forgive, forget, and move on.

10. FAST FROM TV, MAGAZINES, INTERNET, AND SOCIAL MEDIA

   Between all the bad news in the world, unrealistically Photoshopped models in magazines that make us feel bad about ourselves, Internet information overload, and the preoccupation we have with our smartphones, it's a good idea to take a break every now and then from all sources of media. Live in the real world and stop staring at screens all the time. Leave your smartphone at home and hit the beach with friends. Talk about real life, look at real people's bodies, get some sun, and get grounded.

Raw Pitfall: Sugar Overload

A very unfortunate thing happened after I finished writing my first book. My skin started breaking out again. I tried every supplement, skin product, and herbal concoction out there to remedy the situation and was left confused and frustrated. The culprit was right in front of my eyes, and yet I couldn't make the connection for the longest time. It was sugar overload. I had developed candidiasis from all the fruit, agave, dates, goji berries, maple syrup, and dried fruit I was eating. It was throwing off my blood sugar, spiking my insulin, and producing a systemic yeast overgrowth, which was causing a cascade of hormonal and digestive craziness.

Luckily, around the time I was dealing with my acne flare up, I attended a lecture by Donna Gates, author of the book The Body Ecology Diet and an expert at dealing with candida. Gates estimates that 80 percent of the population is suffering from some level of candida overgrowth caused by too much dietary sugar and lack of beneficial microflora in the gut.

Symptoms of candida are many, but here are a few of the major ones:

- Sugar cravings
- Brain fog
- Poor memory
- Low energy
- Irritability
- Acne
- Abdominal bloating
- Gas
- Fatigue
- Migraines
- Respiratory infections
- Iritable bowel syndrome/ disease
- Leaky gut syndrome
- Hormonal imbalances
- Yeast infections

Candida isn't something you can completely eradicate; it's actually a yeast that lives symbiotically throughout the body, in our bloodstream, mouth, throat, and digestive tract. It's part of our bowel flora and can help fight off bad bacteria and pathogens. Candida overgrowth can be kept in check by eating probiotic–rich foods and supplements and by not overconsuming sugar and starchy foods. By taking in lots of good bacteria and starving out the yeast with a low–sugar diet, we can get balanced in as little as one to three months. It's best to continue a low–sugar, high–probiotic, alkaline–rich diet if you have acne or any severe candida symptoms.

I saw tremendous changes in my health when I eliminated all forms of sugar from my diet and increased my daily probiotic intake by eating fermented foods and drinking coconut kefir. Weight loss, clear skin, and the disappearance of PMS symptoms are some of the benefits many women have reported from following these two principles. If you're not finding success on the raw–food diet (or any diet for that matter), eliminate sugar for at least one to three months.

I personally saw great results by following this plan:
- Drinking ¼ cup (60 ml) of coconut kefir every morning
- Eating ½ cup (120 ml) of cultured vegetables with breakfast, lunch, and dinner or drinking ¼ cup (60 ml) of coconut kefir before meals
- Drinking ¼ cup (60 ml) of coconut kefir before bed

I followed this with a sugar–free, high raw diet and had much better skin within three weeks, as well as better blood sugar and digestive and hormonal balance.

This book includes a section on making coconut kefir and cultured vegetables in chapter 3, but you can also easily find them at most health food stores. I recommend Inner Eco coconut kefir and sauerkraut that has been fermented, not pickled in vinegar. Kim chi is also great. Check out my book *Going Raw* for additional fermented recipes.

Anti–Candida Lifestyle Tips

Aside from removing sugars and adding in probiotics, there are many other steps you can take that can help create an inner environment where candida cannot take over.

➤ Alkaline–rich diet. (Hint: You're holding all the information you need about this in your hands.)

➤ Drink plenty of fresh water throughout the day. Start your day with two cups of water with lemon juice and cayenne. This helps stimulate peristalsis in the bowels and flushes out and assists the kidney in the removal of toxic buildup.

➤ Eliminate stress: as it makes your body acidic, weakens the immune system, and elevates cortisol and blood sugar levels—the perfect storm for candida to get out of hand.

➤ Don't overuse antibiotics. Always take extra probiotics if you are prescribed antibiotics, as they will kill all the bacteria in the body, including the beneficial bacteria.

➤ Avoid using birth control pills: The excess estrogen feeds candida.

➤ Keep your bowels moving along by eating a fiber–rich diet. If you are suffering from constipation due to candida, give yourself daily enemas. Two weeks of daily enemas will do wonders for skin conditions, especially acne.

➤ Avoid alcohol, caffeine, dairy, gluten, egg whites, and red meat, all of which aggravate candidiasis.

For an in–depth, step–by–step anti–candida plan, check out www.yeastinfectionnomore.com and *The Body Ecology Diet* by Donna Gates.

Sugar and Insulin

Sugar can wreak havoc in other ways besides feeding candida. Sugar stimulates the pancreas to release insulin, a master hormone whose main function is to escort the blood sugar (glucose) into our cells to be used for energy. Because our SAD diets contain so much sugar and starch, we are releasing insulin several times a day, and that's where it turns into major health problems.

➤ WEIGHT GAIN AND TYPE 2 DIABETES

Too many insulin surges throughout the day can contribute to weight gain and insulin resistance. Excess insulin causes blood sugar levels to drop, leading to strong carbohydrate cravings as the body tries to compensate for the low blood sugar. This makes us reach for the quickest form of energy, usually more sugar, to get balanced, but in doing so we create another blood sugar spike, leading to more insulin, which results in another blood sugar plunge, leading to more ravenous cravings. It's a vicious cycle that I experienced when I used to eat pasta, cake, and other refined carbohydrate foods. The cycle of sugar cravings and blood sugar fluctuations leads to insulin resistance, where your cells no longer respond to the presence of insulin, forcing your pancreas to release even more. Eventually the insulin will tell the liver to store the excess sugar we've been eating as fat. This chain reaction is eventually what leads to obesity, type 2 diabetes, and accelerated aging. Luckily, type 2 diabetes can be reversed by correcting the diet. The documentary *Simply Raw: Reversing Diabetes in 30 Days* shows how six diabetics were able to reverse their condition by eating a sugar–free, raw–food diet.

➤ HORMONAL EFFECTS

Insulin resistance affects every hormone process in the body directly or indirectly. In men, excess insulin converts testosterone into estrogen, which creates abdominal fat (e.g., the beer belly), as well as male breasts. For women, insulin resistance has been connected to estrogen dominance, which can lead to polycystic ovary syndrome (PCOS), fibroids, and excess facial hair. For acne suffers, too much insulin stimulates androgens, which makes our sebaceous glands overactive leading to excess sebum on the skin, which clogs the pores.

➤ HALTED PRODUCTION OF HUMAN GROWTH HORMONE (HGH)

Excess insulin also prevents the body from producing HGH. This anti–aging hormone helps burn fat, build muscle, and improve brain function. Living a lifestyle that keeps HGH levels high will keep you looking and feeling your best. See pages 18–19 for how to up your levels naturally.

➤ FEEDS CANCER CELLS

In 1931, German doctor and Nobel laureate Otto Warburg discovered that cancer cells feed on blood glucose, and there is much evidence to support that removing sugar from the diet may slow tumor growth. In fact, it takes years before cancer actually manifests as a tumor in our body, so the sooner we correct our diets the better chance we have of preventing it. With the amount of radiation we are exposed to in the Northern Hemisphere from the nuclear fallout of Fukushima and the toxic heavy metals in our water, food, and air, we need to do all we can to protect ourselves from the onslaught of environmental cellular damage. By removing excess sugar from our diet, drinking green juices daily, and eating a clean, raw and alkaline diet, we can protect ourselves from this epidemic disease.

The Low–Sugar Lifestyle

Exercise and diet are the two major components to having a low–sugar lifestyle.

➤ EXERCISE

Exercise helps make our cells more receptive to insulin, so make it a part of your daily routine. Moving for at least twenty minutes a day will help stabilize blood sugar balance.

➤ DIET

If you're still eating foods containing high–fructose corn syrup, then stop. Now. Also eliminate refined flour, white rice, and beer and start eating a natural, whole–foods diet high in raw foods. Following a low–sugar/anti–candida diet while trying to eat 100 percent raw is totally doable. The only difficulty is that when you remove fruit, you need to get calories from somewhere else, namely from fats. I didn't like the way eating more fat made me feel, so instead I added gently cooked vegetables, squashes, root vegetables, and quinoa (pronounced *KEEN–wah*), an easy–to–digest, protein–packed alkalizing seed grain. It was easy to adapt many of my recipes from *Going Raw* to make them Body Ecology Diet (BED) friendly. I used alternative sweeteners such as xylitol and stevia in my recipes instead of agave nectar and dates. The recipes in this book give you plenty of wiggle room to modify recipes as you see fit and use sweeteners that work for you.

I hope I'm not making you sugar–phobic. A little is totally okay, but you need to know your personal limit. If you have blood sugar fluctuations, cravings, or get sleepy from eating sweets and refined carbohydrates, then you are better off without it. If you love your green fruit smoothies like I do, focus on low–sugar fruits such as strawberries, blueberries, raspberries, blackberries, acai, and apples, and add as many leafy greens to it as you can tolerate. The fiber from the greens along with the protein and minerals will help keep your blood sugar levels steady. A little tip: Take a probiotic or drink kefir beforehand so the good bacteria can eat up the sugars. You can even add kefir to your smoothies.

CHAPTER TWO

THE RAW & 2 SIMPLE KITCHEN

The best advice I could give on making raw food is always buy the highest-quality ingredients. My pantry is stocked with the freshest organic produce, seeds, and nuts, the finest gourmet seasonings, and gorgeous, small-batch, cold-pressed oils. Since we're not adding any heat to our food to alter the taste, we are left with only the true, naked flavor of our ingredients, so buy the very best whenever you can. You may not be a professional gourmet chef, but you sure can act like one in your kitchen.

Shopping Tips

> BUY ORGANIC

Organic fruits and vegetables have been shown to contain much higher mineral content due to the better quality of soil they are grown in. They are also grown without the use of poisonous pesticides, herbicides, and fungicides. Over one billion tons of toxic pesticides are used every year in the United States alone. Many of them are carcinogenic while others are endocrine disrupters that block or mimic hormones and disrupt normal functions of the body. One very sinister pesticide called methyl iodide, a registered carcinogen, has been linked to neurological damage, miscarriages, and thyroid tumors and is used on vine-growing fruits and vegetables, such as strawberries, tomatoes, peppers, and cucumbers. It mimics iodine and is absorbed into the thyroid where it can wreak havoc—very scary considering thyroid cancer and disease has been rising exponentially in this country. To make it worse, not all pesticides will wash off in the kitchen sink when you take the produce home. Fungicides added to the soil are absorbed into the plants, especially root vegetables, and cannot be removed. Of course, not everyone can afford to eat organic all the time, but you can choose certain produce that is less contaminated than others. Check out the Clean 15 and the Dirty Dozen at the Environmental Working Group website, www.ewg.org. Sign up for their newsletters and get involved with the clean-food movement. By buying organic you support farmers who care about the environment, our health, and the quality of our food, and you will protect yourself and your family from these harmful chemicals. How can you tell if the food you're buying is organic? Read the little stickers on your produce. If the sticker has a four-digit number starting with a 3 or a 4, it's conventionally grown. If it has a five-digit number beginning with a 9, it's organic.

> BUY LOCAL

Most produce is picked weeks before it is ripe, travels many miles, and then is blasted with ethylene gas right before it hits the store shelves to quickly ripen it. If you want to get the freshest food for the best price, then your local farmer's market is your best source. Produce is picked from the farm that morning and sold for less than you will pay at the grocery store. There are also community-supported agriculture (CSA) programs that you can join that will supply you with locally grown produce in season. These buying groups are a way to invest in local farms and guarantee farmers that their crops will be purchased. They are very affordable, and you get a lot of bang for your buck when the crops are harvested. There are also many weekly produce delivery services that will bring a box of fresh produce to your door. You can often tailor these boxes to include more vegetables or more fruit, and you can request certain items to not be included. They're also very affordable and will save you an extra trip to the market. In Southern California, we have several of these delivery services. I have one in my hometown called Beachgreens that gets all its produce from small local, organic, and sustainable farms. I get beautiful, heirloom varieties of produce I would never see at a typical grocery store, and it feels like Christmas every week when I open the box!

> BUY SEASONALLY

Besides the better flavor and cheaper price of buying seasonally, there is something to eating the foods that Mother Nature provides for us at certain times of the year. In springtime, nature gives us cleansing foods such as tender leafy greens, grapefruits, lemons, oranges, berries, and dandelion. This is an excellent time to do a detox such as a juice fast. In the summer, nature gives us cooling foods like watermelon, peaches, tomatoes, cucumber, and zucchini. This is an ideal time to try a 100 percent raw diet. In autumn and winter, we get grounding and warming foods like beets, carrots, onions, garlic, sweet potatoes, squashes, and cruciferous vegetables such as cabbage, kale, and Brussels sprouts. (Of course, this will vary depending on where you live.) Eating seasonally is an ancient Eastern tradition that connects us to our location and the rhythm of nature's cycles, and gets us more in tune with our body, which results in better health.

> AVOID GMOS

Genetically modified organisms, or GMOs, are slowly creeping into our food supply. If the large biotechnology corporations have their way, they will be able to continue tampering with our food without our knowledge. By splicing together genes from bacterium and genes of plants, these companies can create pest- or drought-resistant frankenfoods that nature never intended. GMOs have never been tested on humans, but laboratory studies have shown animals that eat genetically engineered food become infertile by the third generation. GMOs have also been shown to cause liver damage, organ failure, allergies, digestive bleeding, and birth defects. Currently, the law does not require GMOs to be labeled so it's important to know what foods to avoid. As of right now, the majority of corn, soy, canola, cottonseed, and Hawaiian papaya is genetically modified. Corn, soy, and canola are found in many prepackaged and processed foods, so check the labels before you buy. Soon, genetically engineered alfalfa, tomatoes, chicory, flax, potato, rice, sugar beets, apples, and squash will be filling the store shelves as well. This is another great reason to buy organic and become a champion for clean, safe food. I highly recommend watching the documentary *The Future of Food* to find out more about how Monsanto and other biotech companies are trying to control the global food supply.

Just the Basics: Stocking Your Pantry

Here are a few of the staples used regularly in this book. Health food stores will be your best source for organic ingredients. You can also find good deals online. Visit my store at www.rawjudita.com for some hard-to-find items.

➤ FRUITS:

Look for fresh, unbruised fruit. I rarely buy frozen fruit, but if I have an excess, I'll freeze or juice it.

- Lemons
- Limes
- Apples
- Oranges
- Bananas
- Avocados
- Young Thai coconuts
- And a little bit of whatever is currently in season

➤ VEGETABLES AND LEAFY GREENS:

Avoid precut, prepackaged vegetables that have been sitting in plastic bags and containers for who knows how long. Instead pick loose, vibrant-looking vegetables, and buy only as much as you will use in five to seven days.

- Kale
- Spinach
- Mesclun or spring mix
- Cucumbers
- Celery
- Carrots
- Zucchini
- Onions (red, white, yellow)
- Tomatoes
- Bell peppers (red, orange, and yellow; not green— they're unripe!)

➤ HERBS:

I grow many herbs in my garden and on my kitchen windowsill. It's much more economical than buying them at the store, and they're pretty to look at. I use these the most.

- Basil
- Mint
- Cilantro
- Parsley
- Thyme
- Oregano
- Dill

➤ RAW NUTS AND SEEDS:

Raw nuts go rancid quickly, so buy only a month's worth.

- Almonds
- Walnuts
- Cashews
- Hazelnuts
- Pine nuts
- Chia seeds
- Hemp seeds
- Pumpkin seeds
- Sunflower seeds

➤ GRAINS:

These are the only grains used in this book.

- Gluten-free whole oat groats
- Gluten-free rolled oats

➤ NUT AND SEED BUTTERS:

You can find raw nut butters at most health food stores. Once opened, refrigerate and use within two months.

- Almond butter
- Unroasted tahini

➤ OILS:

Look for organic, cold-pressed, extra-virgin oils to get the best flavor and highest nutrient content. The best seed oils on the market are Andreas brand.

- Olive oil
- Flaxseed oil
- Hazelnut oil
- Unrefined coconut oil

➤ SALTS:

Toss the chemically processed, iodized salt and instead use a trace mineral-rich, natural sea salt or pink salt.

- Celtic sea salt
- Himalayan pink salt

➤ SEA VEGETABLES:

I recommend checking the source before buying. North Atlantic seaweeds are the least contaminated at this time. Here are my favorites.

- Raw nori sheets
- Dulse flakes or pieces
- Arame

➤ SPICES AND FLAVORINGS:

You certainly don't need to buy everything on this list, but they do bring a variety of great flavors to raw foods. When purchasing dried herbs, buy small quantities and replace them every six months.

- Apple cider vinegar (raw, unfiltered)
- Balsamic vinegar
- Nutritional yeast
- Nama shoyu or tamari (fermented, traditionally brewed soy sauces)
- Sweet, white, or chickpea miso paste
- Wholegrain Dijon mustard
- Fresh garlic
- Fresh ginger
- Vanilla beans
- Vanilla extract (I prefer alcohol-free from Frontier Foods)
- Sun-dried tomatoes (dry, not packed in oil)
- Black or white sesame seeds
- Capers
- Dried olives
- Cacao powder and nibs
- Untoasted carob powder
- Clove powder
- Whole nutmeg
- Cinnamon sticks
- Black and white pepper
- Garlic powder
- Onion powder
- Cumin
- Cardamom
- Paprika
- Chipotle chili powder
- Cayenne pepper
- Crushed red pepper
- Turmeric
- Pumpkin pie spice blend
- Italian seasoning blend
- Curry seasoning blend
- Mexican chili powder
- Garam masala

➤ SUN-DRIED FRUITS:

Avoid dried fruit containing sulfur dioxide, vegetables oils, or sugar.

- Raisins
- Medjool dates
- Cranberries
- Apples
- Cherries
- Goji berries
- Dried shredded coconut (unsweetened)

➤ SWEETENERS:

I use various sweeteners, but these are my go-tos for their versatility and neutral or unique flavor.

- Agave nectar (clear)
- Xylitol
- Stevia (liquid)
- Maple syrup (grade B)
- Raw honey

Note: Some ingredients in this book are not 100 percent raw, such as maple syrup and rolled oats. I'm not a raw-food puritan, so bending the rules doesn't bother me, especially since they're still full of good minerals and incredibly tasty!

Equipment

You don't need to go out and buy special, expensive equipment to get started with raw food. You probably already have everything you need, but a few gadgets here and there can make things easier. Here's a list of some raw–food kitchen basics I keep in my kitchen.

➤ A GOOD KNIFE:

You're going to do a lot of slicing and dicing so get yourself a good–quality 8–inch (20 cm) chef's knife. A paring knife is also handy, as is a knife sharpener (more accidents happen with a dull knife than a sharp one).

➤ CUTTING BOARD:

I like wood and bamboo boards with a large surface area.

➤ MEASURING CUPS AND SPOONS:

Get a set of dry measuring cups as well as a liquid measuring cup and a set of measuring spoons.

➤ MIXING BOWLS:

Small, medium, and large bowls to help you make your raw creations.

➤ HANDY UTENSILS:

These include things like a rubber spatula, peeler, whisk, small offset spatula, mixing spoon, hand grater, julienne slicer, strainer/colander, sushi mat, citrus reamer, spice grinder, and squeeze bottle.

➤ MICROPLANE:

This one is optional. This long, fine grater is excellent for mincing garlic and grating zest and spices, and is one of my favorite gadgets in the kitchen.

➤ NUT MILK BAG:

This reusable nylon bag is used to strain nut pulp when making nondairy nut milk.

➤ MASON JARS AND STORAGE CONTAINERS:

I use quart–size mason jars to soak nuts and store sauces and ingredients, and I drink my smoothies out of them, too. A variety of different storage containers are essential. I prefer to use glass containers over plastic.

➤ SPIRALIZER:

This fun little contraption will turn zucchini, daikon radish, carrots, and other vegetables into spaghetti noodles.

➤ MANDOLINE:

This will cut your vegetables into paper–thin slices. It's a big time saver, but you can always do it by hand.

➤ ICE POP MAKER:

This one is optional, but I have several ice pop recipes that fit the Norpo Frozen Ice Pop Maker, though any brand will work. You can even use an ice cube tray for your ice pops.

➤ MINI CUPCAKE PAN:

This is optional though very helpful to make my cupcake recipes. They keep the shape much better, but you can bypass it and just press dough carefully into the wrappers by hand.

➤ PASTRY BAG:

This optional tool makes icing your cupcakes a breeze, but a little butter knife and some patience will work, too.

➤ FOOD PROCESSOR:

A seven–cup (1.6 liter) food processor is big enough to handle everything in this book. I use only the S blade for my recipes, but a shredding blade is also really handy for prepping large amounts of vegetables.

➤ BLENDER:

A high–speed blender like a Vitamix or Blendtec is a treat to own and a worthwhile investment if you love working in the kitchen. You can make the silkiest sauces and creams as well as gelatos and nut butters, but, unfortunately, these blenders can be a bit pricey. A conventional blender will do just fine starting out, but it may mean a bit more effort and the results may not be as smooth. A mini blender is also handy for making small batches—it's not essential but nice to have.

➤ JUICER:

Get a juicer that can handle everything from fruits and vegetables to leafy greens. I've had an Omega 8005 for years. It's an all–purpose machine, but a little slow and clunky. Faster juicers are convenient, but the speed oxidizes the nutrients, so it's a bit of tradeoff with whichever one you go with. If you have only a blender, you can process your fruits and veggies with a little bit of water and then squeeze the liquid through a nut milk bag to make juice.

➤ DEHYDRATOR:

I've made the recipes in this book dehydrator–free, but if you own one, use it to warm your raw dishes. My book *Going Raw* contains delicious recipes that call for a dehydrator.

Techniques, Tips, and Tricks

You don't have to go to culinary school to become a proficient raw food home chef. Here are a few easy techniques and tips to help you with the recipes in this book. It might be a little slow going at first, but with a bit of practice you will be a pro in no time!

➤ SPIRALIZING VEGETABLES

Turning your veggies into noodles is a breeze with a spiralizer. It's best to use vegetables that are straight and don't contain a lot of seeds like cucumbers or very large zucchinis. I prefer spiralizers that make thicker spaghetti–like noodles instead of very fine angel hair because the larger noodles release less water. If you don't own a spiralizer yet, you can make ribbons using a vegetable peeler.

➤ VANILLA BEANS

I love using fresh vanilla beans, but they can be somewhat pricey if you buy them individually. I've seen single beans selling for $10 when I get them for around $0.50 each by buying them in bulk. Check the resources section (page 169) for suggestions on where to buy them and save big time. You can also find vanilla powder, which is whole vanilla beans grounded down. A little goes a long way so start off small or it may overtake your dish.

To scrape a fresh vanilla bean, use a paring knife to make a slit down the middle without cutting all the way through. Use the tip of the knife to open up the bean and expose the seeds. Use the side of the knife to scrape out seeds. I steep leftover pods in teas or dry them out and grind them into vanilla powder.

➤ SOAKING NUTS AND SEEDS

Soaking nuts and seeds not only makes them easier to blend, but it also removes the enzyme inhibitors that make seeds and nuts dormant. Removing the enzyme inhibitors decreases some of the acidity and bitterness and makes them easier to digest. Brazil nuts, cashews, and hazelnuts do not have enzyme inhibitors, but soaking them will help them blend better if you don't have a high–power blender. I recommend soaking them for two hours, but it's not totally necessary.

Soak nuts by putting them in a bowl and covering them with water. You can either leave them on the counter or in the refrigerator. I prefer to leave mine on the counter so I don't forget about them.

Soak times will depend on which nuts you use. You can also use seeds or a combination of both.

Soaking Time

- Brazil nuts: 2 hours
- Almonds: 8–12 hours
- Cashews: 2 hours
- Hazelnuts: 2 hours
- Pecans: 4–6 hours
- Pumpkin seeds: 4–6 hours
- Walnuts: 6–8 hours
- Hemp seeds: None (not necessary to soak)

➤ THE RAW DEAL ON RAW NUTS

In 2008, the FDA required all almonds grown in the United States to be pasteurized to prevent salmonella contamination. Under this new law, almond growers were still allowed to label the almonds raw, though, technically, they are no longer a living, sproutable seed. Since then, many nut growers have pasteurized via gas, steam, or irradiation not only their almonds, but almost all nuts. Raw nuts purchased at most chain grocers are pretty much all pasteurized. This is unfortunate, but it doesn't mean it's all bad. Pasteurized nuts still contain healthy fats and minerals. The good news is imported nuts, such as Italian almonds, do not have be pasteurized, and there is a loophole for U.S. farmers to be able to sell raw nuts directly to consumers. You can find truly raw nuts on some raw food websites, and many offer great deals on bulk purchases.

➤ YOUNG THAI COCONUTS (shown above)

Two popular types of coconuts are available at most health food stores and Asian markets: the iconic fuzzy brown coconuts and the young Thai coconuts. The latter are the white–husked coconuts with cut, cone–shaped tops usually found in the refrigerated produce section.

Mature coconuts have very thick dry meat and little water, while young Thai coconuts have a small amount of soft meat and contain 1 to 2 cups (235–353 ml) of water. Look for ones with a soft, spongy husk and no dark purple spots or cracks on the bottom. Only young Thai coconuts are used for the recipes in this book.

Opening Young Thai Coconuts

There are two ways to open a coconut. I recommend getting a good–size cleaver as well as a sturdy chef's knife.

IMPORTANT: Stay focused when using a cleaver. Do not raise your arm above your head or leave your fingers exposed anywhere near the target.

➤ THE QUICK METHOD:

Place coconut on a hard, flat surface. Use a cleaver (and your burly muscles) to make four deep cuts into the top of the cone. Keep your hands off the coconut, ok? It's quick, easy and most of the time not messy. Remove the top and skip down to step 4.

➤ THE EASY METHOD:

1. Use a sharp knife to remove the husk from the top portion of the coconut, exposing the brown nut.

2. Turn the coconut on its side and hold it firmly from the bottom. With the heel of a sharp cleaver, aim for the outermost part of the exposed nut and give it a firm whack. It may take a few tries, depending on the coconut.

3. Once you have the heel firmly in the nut, turn the coconut back on its base and lift the cleaver to create a flap. This will happen very naturally as the crack will always (ok, usually) create a perfect circle.

4. Pour the coconut water through a fine strainer before using to remove any shell pieces.

5. The water should be clear or slightly cloudy and sweet. If it is purple, very cloudy, or smells off, you should discard the whole coconut. Always do a taste test before using the coconut or coconut water in a recipe.

6. Store the water in the refrigerator and use within three days.

Scraping

1. Use a rubber spatula to scrape out the meat. Depending on how young the coconut is, you will have meat ranging from very gelatinous to thick and firm.

2. Remove any bits of shell with a paring knife.

3. Coconut meat stores very well. Keep it in the freezer until you're ready to use it.

To Make Coconut Milk

1. Add the coconut water and scraped meat of the coconut into a high–power blender and process until smooth. If the coconut milk comes out too watery or looks speckled add additional coconut meat (from another coconut) until it has a consistent, milky (not speckled) texture (it will be a little thicker than canned, store bought coconut milk).

2. Coconut milk is great to use in smoothies, desserts, soups, and sauces. I use it in several of the recipes in this book, including the Carrot Ginger Coconut Soup (page 77) and Cocojito (page 63).

➤ FOOD STORAGE

Fruit:

Some foods are best left on the countertop such as tomatoes, nectarines, peaches, pears, plums, watermelon, citrus fruits, unripe bananas and other tropical fruit, and avocados. Ripen tropical fruit on the counter and then move it to the refrigerator. When avocados are fully ripe, stick them in the refrigerator where they'll keep for another two to three days. Foods that spoil the fastest are avocados, bananas, basil, cherries, corn, dill, mushrooms, strawberries, and watercress. Eat them within two to three days of buying them.

Leafy greens:

To keep your herbs and leafy greens from getting sad and slimy, wash them in cold water, pat them mostly dry, and wrap them in paper towels. I like storing them in Everett green bags, but a regular plastic bag will do. This will keep them fresh for up to one week.

Vegetables:

Most vegetables can be stored in a plastic bag in the refrigerator for several days, such as broccoli, cauliflower, cucumbers, celery, green onions, peppers, beets, carrots, and summer squash. Remove tops of beets and carrots. Store tops like leafy greens and use them in salads and juices.

Garlic and onions:

Store in the pantry away from heat and light.

Berries:

Store berries in the refrigerator, unwashed, in their original container.

Mushrooms:

Store in a paper bag in the refrigerator.

Oils:

Olive, flax, and other seed oils should be kept in the refrigerator and away from light. They go rancid quickly, so use them within one month of opening. Coconut oil is very shelf stable and can last for several weeks in your pantry.

Nuts and seeds:

I store them in the refrigerator to maintain their freshness.

Oats:

Oats will last three months in an airtight container in the cupboard or six months if stored in the refrigerator.

Seaweeds:

Store in an airtight container in the cupboard to retain freshness.

Note: Freshen up your limp greens, celery, carrots, and green onions by trimming off whatever doesn't need reviving. Submerge in a sink or bowl of ice cold water for several minutes. Shake off excess water but do not dry completely. Loosely wrap in paper towels and place in a plastic bag and return to the refrigerator. They should perk up in two to three hours.

➤ BLENDING TIPS

Place liquid ingredients into the blender first, followed by solid and dry ingredients. This will help get the blades moving.

The friction from high power blenders can heat up your food. This is great if you're making a soup, but if the blender motor gets too hot by running excessively, it will shut down for 15 minutes or more depending on what brand you're using.

For easy clean up, fill with water and a squirt of dish soap, blend, and rinse.

➤ FOOD PROCESSOR TIPS

Food processors are better for blending solid foods while a blender is better suited for liquids.

Use the "Pulse" button to quickly chop your ingredients or use the "On" button to blend and homogenize ingredients.

You may need to stop and start your mixture if it starts to creep up the sides. Scrape down the sides of the container and push ingredients toward the blade as needed.

The Raw Food Groups

Think you'll starve on a raw-food diet? You won't! Here's an overview of many of the delicious fare that you can enjoy.

➤ FRUITS

Fruits are loaded with vitamins, minerals, phytonutrients, and simple sugars to fuel our cells. On a raw-food diet, you'll enjoy apples, oranges, strawberries, pineapples, papaya, bananas, apricots, plums, dates, dried fruits.

➤ VEGETABLES

Vegetables are low in calories and full of fiber, so you can eat as much as you like. Munch on cucumbers, celery, bell peppers, tomatoes, beets, zucchini, broccoli, cauliflower, peas, corn, and so on.

➤ LEAFY GREENS

Green leaves are essential to a raw food diet because they contain essential minerals such as calcium, iron, and magnesium, and are a great source of protein and blood-building chlorophyll. Green and red leaf lettuce, kale, spinach, collards, Swiss chard, romaine, bok choy, watercress, arugula, dandelion, and lambsquarters are a few leafy green all-stars.

➤ SEEDS

Pumpkin, sunflower, hemp, flax, chia, and sesame seeds are a great source of protein, minerals and essential fatty acids.

➤ NUTS

Almonds, cashews, Brazil nuts, walnuts, pecans, pine nuts, hazelnuts, pistachios, wild jungle peanuts, and macadamia nuts all contain heart-healthy fats, protein, and minerals.

➤ GRAINS

Oats, kamut, spelt, quinoa, buckwheat, and hand-parched wild rice can all be prepared raw. In this book we will only be using oats, the easiest one to prepare.

➤ SPROUTS

Alfalfa, sunflower, broccoli, clover, mung beans, chickpeas, lentils, and quinoa are just a few types of sprouts you can grow at home and enjoy in salads and wraps. See my first book, *Going Raw*, for information on how to grow your own sprouts.

➤ FERMENTED FOODS

Fermented foods contain high amounts of beneficial bacteria that help improve our digestion and strengthen our immune system. Sauerkraut and cultured vegetables, kombucha, water, coconut and kefir, almond and coconut yogurt, and miso paste are all part of a raw-food diet.

➤ FATS

Avocados, coconuts, and sun-dried olives as well as oils such as coconut, flaxseed, hemp seed, sacha inchi, and olive oil are all healthy fats. Make sure oils are cold-pressed (not expeller-pressed) and extra virgin.

Note: DO avoid peanut oil, which is refined and may cause allergic reactions, and raw sunflower and safflower oils, which contain too much inflammatory omega-6. Also avoid canola, soybean, and corn oil, because they are very processed and may come from genetically modified crops.

➤ SEA VEGETABLES

There are at least two dozen edible seaweeds, but my favorites are dulse, kelp, nori, wakame, and arame. They're full of essential trace minerals and amino acids and have great radiation-protecting qualities.

➤ SUPERFOODS

Superfoods have exceptionally high concentrations of nutrients and unique properties. There are many out there, but my favorites are goji berries, maca powder, bee pollen, blue-green algae, marine phytoplankton, and cacao. See page 34–35 for more on superfoods.

➤ SWEETENERS

Clear agave nectar, palm sugar, raw honey, stevia, yacon syrup, mesquite powder, xylitol, erythritol, lucuma, maple syrup, and dehydrated cane juice (rapadura) all naturally add sweetness. Except for raw honey, dried stevia leaf, lucuma, and mesquite, most sugars are processed to some extent and are not considered truly raw, even if they are labeled as such. Avoid white processed sugar, sugar in the raw, and turbinado sugar, which are all stripped of their minerals. Also steer clear of all artificial sweeteners such as aspartame, sucralose, and saccharin.

An Overview of Alternative Sweeteners

There are many different alternative sweeteners on the market that you can use in your raw creations. Most are processed to some degree, but I have found the ones listed here to be the best and safest choice for the conscious chef.

➤ STEVIA

This sweetener comes from the stevia plant, whose leaves can be dried and ground into a green, all-natural powder. It's intensely sweet with a bitter, licorice-like aftertaste. It also comes in a processed white powder form as well as a liquid. I prefer to use liquid stevia in my recipes and find it works best in beverages. It has no side effects, no impact on blood sugar, and is safe for diabetics, cancer patients, and those on a candida-elimination diet. A little goes a long way, so use it sparingly. I like to use Stevia Botanica and Sweetleaf brands in my recipes.

➤ AGAVE NECTAR

Once the king of natural sweeteners, this sweet, neutral-tasting liquid has been criticized in some health circles for being worse than high-fructose corn syrup as it, too, is composed mostly of fructose. I find that to be rather alarmist since agave is minimally processed from the succulent agave plant while high-fructose corn syrup is a highly processed refined sugar made from genetically modified corn. Fruit also contains fructose, but no one is saying we should avoid fruit like the plague. Quality is important, though. The agave nectar you want to look for is *clear*. You will find many amber shades of agave labeled as raw because fructose will caramelize at 110°F (43°C). This is below the 118°F (48°C) raw limit so companies feel they can go ahead and call it raw, though it has clearly gone through a chemical change. Since some people have an aversion to it, I'm not using it as much in this book, but I have included it in recipes where I think it works the best compared to other sweeteners.

➤ XYLITOL

Xylo is Greek for wood, from which this sweetener is mostly harvested. It is a zero-glycemic, crystallized sugar alcohol that has no effect on blood sugar and does not contribute to bacteria and yeast growth, making it a great option for diabetics and candida sufferers. I use this sweetener quite a bit as it tastes very much like sucrose and works magnificently in desserts. I chose to use this sweetener the most in this book because it is easy to find in most health food stores. It's perfectly safe and has no major side effects, though a laxative effect may occur with overconsumption. If you're sensitive to it, then I recommend trying erythritol instead.

➤ ERYTHRITOL

This crystallized sweetener, extracted by fermenting fruit sugars, is very similar to xylitol. It's also a zero-glycemic sugar alcohol and is a bit less sweet than sucrose. It is absorbed into the bloodstream from the stomach, not the intestines, so it will not cause any digestive disturbances. If you would like to use it instead of xylitol, you will need a little bit more of it to achieve the same amount of sweetness.

➤ YACON SYRUP

This low-glycemic, thick, molasses-like syrup is made from the tuberous roots of the yacon plant. Because it comes from the ground, it is very mineral rich and also contains 50 percent fructooligosaccharides, short-chain fructose molecules that are not digested by the body and have no impact on blood sugar. It is also a prebiotic, as it helps feed beneficial bacteria. Yacon syrup has half the calories of sugar and is diabetic friendly. I use organic yacon syrup by Navitas Naturals.

➤ MAPLE SYRUP

I use this delicious, mineral-rich sweetener to enhance the flavor of desserts and granolas. It does impact blood sugar and feeds bacteria and yeast so avoid it if you are diabetic or following an anti-candida or anticancer diet.

➤ COCONUT PALM SUGAR

A light-brown crystallized sweetener made from the evaporated nectar of palm trees, coconut palm sugar is minimally processed and contains an array of minerals and vitamins. It is lower on the glycemic index than agave or honey and tastes delicious. Avoid it if you are following an anti-candida or anticancer diet.

➤ EVAPORATED CANE JUICE

This is a minimally processed form of sugar that still has the nutrients intact from the sugar cane. It's a brown, grainy sweetener that is wonderful to use in raw piecrusts and other desserts. It's a much better alternative to refined sugar, but avoid it if you are diabetic or on an anti-candida or anticancer program.

➤ HONEY

Though not a vegan product, honey does have wonderful healing properties and comes in many different floral varieties. Make sure the label says unfiltered and raw. Do not give it to babies and avoid it if you are on a low-sugar, anticandida, or anticancer program.

➤ DATES

You can sweeten many recipes with dates. They're all natural and full of minerals. My favorite dates are Medjool dates, which are large, soft and caramel-like. Avoid if you are on a low-sugar, anticandida, or anticancer program.

Though some recipes are specific about which sweetener to use, many allow you to choose your sweetener of choice. Sometimes I like to use a combination of two different sweeteners, like a few drops of stevia along with agave.

Superfoods

There are some foods that are so health–promoting, they deserve their own category. These foods usually have exceptionally high phytonutrient and antioxidant content or other nutritional benefits. The following are the rock stars of the raw–food world. Even though I don't use all of these in this book, I suggest you experiment with as many as you can. They are easy to incorporate into your cooked dishes as well.

➤ HEMP SEEDS

These rich, nutty seeds will not give you the munchies, nor with they grow into a medicinal plant for your herb collection. But they are full of essential fatty acids like omega–3 and –6 and gamma–linolenic acid, a super–anti–inflammatory fatty acid that helps balance hormones. Hemp seeds are also very high in complete protein. In fact, they are 35 percent digestible protein and an excellent source of major and trace minerals. I enjoy them sprinkled over salads, blended into smoothies, mixed into chocolate treats, or made into a nut milk (page 59).

➤ GOJI BERRIES

These pretty, red berries have been used as a tonic herb in traditional Chinese medicine for centuries. Considered an *adaptogen*, a term used to describe herbs that have therapeutic effects on the body, goji berries have been known to support the liver, kidney, and adrenals and boost immune function. They contain two to four times the amount of antioxidants found in blueberries and are the only food known to stimulate the body to produce more HGH, making it a great antiaging food. Goji berries also contain all essential amino acids, iron, and other trace minerals. Enjoy them in smoothies, as a snack, over cereal, or in deserts.

➤ CACAO

This delicious bean is very high in antioxidants, heart–protecting magnesium, blood–sugar–balancing chromium, and immune–supporting zinc. It's also high in tryptophan, a mood–enhancing amino acid that is responsible for the production of serotonin, our primary neurotransmitter. Enjoy cacao in powder form or as nibs in smoothies and desserts.

➤ COCONUTS

Coconuts have a host of great health benefits. They contain lauric acid, which your body converts to monolaurin, a compound that is antimicrobial, antifungal, antiparasitic, and antibacterial. Lauric acid is also a medium–chain fatty acid (MCFA) that is easily digested and used as fuel—like carbohydrates but without the insulin spike. MCFAs actually boost your metabolism and help your body burn fat for fuel, helping you get lean and mean. Blend coconut meat and oil into smoothies and desserts. Use coconut oil as a moisturizer, as shaving cream, or in your hair to tame the frizzies.

➤ CHIA SEEDS

You may remember cha–cha–cha–chia pets from when you were younger. Well, now the tiny ancient Latin American chia seeds are making a comeback in a big way. They are an excellent source of essential fatty acids, having ounce for ounce more omega–3 than salmon. Chia is also a complete protein and a great source of calcium, potassium, and fiber. They can help regulate blood sugar, curb your appetite, and provide long–lasting energy. Chia seeds don't have to be ground like flax seeds to get all the nutrients. Add them to smoothies or try them in chia puddings (page 44) or Chia Fresca (page 68).

➤ SPIRULINA

This ancient, single–celled, blue–green spiral algae has existed since the dawn of time. It is the simplest of life forms and contains in it the building blocks of life, as it is the very beginning of the food chain. It grows naturally in warm, alkaline lakes and ponds and has been eaten as a food for five thousand years. It has a higher concentration of protein (59 percent to 71 percent) than any other plant food and has as much iron as red meat. It is also rich in vitamins, chlorophyll, phytonutrients, and enzymes. Buy it as a powder and use it in smoothies and dressings, sprinkle it over salads, or add it to raw dark chocolate desserts.

➤ CHLORELLA:

Like spirulina, chlorella is a single–celled microalgae. It gets its name from the high amount of chlorophyll it possesses. It is also rich in vitamins, minerals, amino acids, essential fatty acids, and phytonutrients. Its superpower is that it is a great detoxifier, clearing heavy metals, pesticides, and other toxic compounds from the body's tissues. It's also a great liver and blood cleanser and improves immune function in people undergoing chemotherapy. It also has an unusual ability to multiply the growth rate of lactobacillus (beneficial bacteria) in our stomach and intestines, thereby improving digestion and assimilation of nutrients. Chlorella can be taken as a powder or pressed tablets. The tablets are actually really tasty to chew on but will turn your mouth bright green. Don't chew on them before a big date!

➤ MACA

Maca root is grown high in the Peruvian Andes. It is harvested, dried, and ground into a powder. It has been enjoyed for the past 2,600 years for its libido–enhancing properties as well as for improving strength and stamina. Like goji berries, it is an adaptogen and has the ability to balance the body's glandular–hormonal, nervous, and cardiovascular systems. It's been known to improve problems with anemia, stress, chronic fatigue, depression, fertility, thyroid issues, PMS, and menopausal symptoms. Use powdered maca in smoothies and desserts.

➤ BEE POLLEN

One of the most complete foods found in nature, bee pollen contains all twenty–two amino acids, eighteen vitamins, fourteen fatty acids, and an array of minerals, enzymes, and antioxidants, as well as having aphrodisiac and fertility–improving properties. Athletes can benefit from increased strength, endurance, energy, and speed by taking bee pollen. Enjoy it in smoothies, elixirs, desserts, or by itself.

➤ ACAI

This little bluish–purple berry comes from the Amazon rainforests of Brazil. It contains high levels of essential fatty acids and is remarkably rich in antioxidants and sterols. It is high in minerals and vitamins, including calcium, phosphorus, beta carotene, and vitamin E. Acai might be helpful in the prevention of cancer, as its ability to neutralize free radicals is extraordinary. Recent research has also shown that acai can help regenerate and produce stem cells. You can find it in a freeze–dried powder or as a puree in the freezer section of your health–food store. Blend these superfoods into smoothies or use in desserts.

➤ CAMU CAMU BERRIES

These berries are native to the South American rainforest. They contain thirty times more vitamin C than oranges and are an excellent source of calcium, phosphorus, potassium, and iron. They're great for boosting the immune system and creating beautiful skin and strong tendons, as vitamin C is essential for the synthesis of collagen. They're also great for warding off viral infections, decreasing inflammation, and maintaining excellent eyesight. You can buy camu camu powder and add it to water, juice, smoothies, or desserts. I stave off colds and sore throats by drinking a teaspoon mixed in water several times a day if I have any sign of symptoms. It works like a charm every time.

➤ KELP

This sea vegetable is very rich in minerals including calcium, magnesium, potassium, iron, and iodine, which is essential for thyroid function. It contains phytochemicals that have the ability to absorb and eliminate heavy metals and radioactive elements from the body. Kelp also contains essential sugars that are antibacterial, antifungal, and antiviral. You can buy dried kelp that can be reconstituted in water and added to salad or soups, or you can try kelp granules. The granules can be used as a salt replacement or seasoning.

➤ NONI

If you can get past the smelly gym sock odor, this tropical fruit is a great health–promoting food. It contains powerful antioxidants and is particularly helpful for people with compromised immune systems. Studies show it stimulates white blood cells and makes them more powerful. Fresh noni can boost serotonin levels while fermented noni juice has strong antimicrobial and antifungal properties. Tea from the leaves aids digestion, stabilizes blood sugar levels, eliminates toxins, and doesn't contain the pungent odor of the fruit. You can find the fruit in powdered form at heath stores. Add a little to water, coconut water, or smoothies.

➤ ALOE VERA

Topically, aloe is excellent for healing burns, acne, eczema, insect bites and stings, poison ivy, rashes, skin allergies, and infections. Internally, aloe's antimicrobial properties are great for digestive wellness. It cuts and dissolves mucus in the intestines, allowing it to increase nutrient absorption. It is effective at killing yeast (candida) and increases the presence of friendly bacteria as a prebiotic. It is also able to activate the liver to produce glutathione, a powerful antioxidant essential for the production of white blood cells. Fresh aloe gel is superior to bottled gel. Buy thick aloe leaves without white speckles. You will need to filet them to remove the inner gel, which can be added to smoothies, soups, dips, and salsas.

To learn more about using superfoods in recipes and everyday life, check out two of my favorite books on the topic: *Superfood Kitchen* by Julie Morris and *Superfoods* by David Wolfe.

Raw in a Cooked World

Chances are you're probably the only one in your family interested in following a raw diet. I was and still am the only raw foodist in my family and among my closest friends (though I do have many raw friends around the world!). I didn't have a lot of support when I started my raw diet, but I knew I had to make a change if I wanted to fix my skin problem. I wrote down my goals and was determined to reach them despite the naysayers and the challenges that come about when trying to eat 100 percent fresh foods. I was especially blessed to have a husband who was totally supportive, though he himself wasn't ready to take the 100 percent raw plunge. He saw my frustration with my skin and was on board with supporting me in this new health endeavor. Though there were days I could have killed him for baking a pizza while I was juice fasting, it meant a lot to me to have him cheering me on. Inspired by my success, he eats at least 50 percent raw most days, is an avid surfer, rarely gets sick, and is in peak health at age forty.

➤ TWO BITS OF ADVICE WHEN GOING RAW

1. Ask for support. Explain to your loved ones the goals that you want to reach through this diet. Ask that they support and not judge or criticize your efforts.

2. Don't try to change their diet. People are very attached to the food they eat, so don't try to change someone's diet if he or she isn't ready for it. Better to let people see your great results and be inspired than to push them out of their comfort zone.

➤ INTRODUCING RAW FOOD TO KIDS

Children can be enticed easily with raw foods. Fruit smoothies, ice pops, and raw desserts will not be a problem at all. Getting them to eat raw vegetables, though, might be. Here are some easy tips.

- Explain to kids how different vegetables help them grow into superheroes. For examples, carrots make your eyes see better so you can spot baddies. Broccoli will help you not get sick. Spinach makes you strong like Popeye. (This is what my parents told me growing up and it worked.)

- Sneak some mild greens into their smoothies, but add some blueberries so the color isn't so…green.
- Let them help you prepare raw recipes.
- Plant a garden with them so they learn where food comes from. They will get a total thrill out of eating food that they grew themselves.

➤ ACCOMMODATING A COOKED FAMILY

If you have to go it alone, you will probably have to make food both for yourself and for your family. Integrate some of the raw recipes from this book into family meals by adding raw soups and salads alongside cooked dishes. Here are some recipes that are very family friendly:

- Cherry–Hemp Muesli with Vanilla Cashew–Hemp Milk (page 44)
- Southwest Corn Chowder (page 73)
- Nacho Cheese Sauce (page 86)
- Smoky Guacamole (page 86)
- Red Bell Pepper Hummus (page 85)
- Five Pepper Chili (page 129)
- Zucchini Pasta Marinara (page 126)
- Watermelon-Tomato Salad (page 107)
- Colorful Cabbage Salad (page 99)
- Any of the fruit smoothies, beverages, and desserts

I've noted specific recipes in this book that can be gently warmed on a stovetop. That way you can keep it raw for yourself and gently cooked for the family.

People often ask me what are some healthy cooked options. I recommend alkalizing, whole foods, such as:

- Steamed greens, vegetables, and squashes
- Sautéed or baked vegetables and squashes (use coconut oil for high–heat cooking)
- Vegetable soups
- Quinoa, a versatile gluten–free pseudo grain (soak overnight before using)
- Lentils, not from a can
- Shirataki noodles made from konjac—a yamlike tuber, not soy

Timesaving Tips

As you get more proficient in the kitchen, the faster you'll be able to put together quick raw meals. Here are a few tips to help you be more efficient so you have more time to relax and enjoy life.

➤ PLANNING TIPS

It's a good idea to have a few basics prepared and on deck so you don't have to constantly be doing food prep every day. Put a couple hours aside once a week to prepare some dressings, sauces, desserts, and so forth at one time so you can relax the rest of the week. I like to put on some good jams while I do my food prep or listen to health lectures to get inspired.

➤ ONCE A WEEK

- Make two salad dressings. They could be any of the dressings from the salad recipes, such as Lemon Tahini (page 127) and Chipotle–Maple Vinaigrette (page 108). (Prep time: 15 minutes)
- Make two to three snack condiments, such as Red Bell Pepper Hummus (page 85), Nacho Cheese (page 86), and Hemp Seed Butter (page 147). (Prep time: about 45 minutes)
- Make two desserts such as Chocolate Haystacks (page 155) and Oatmeal Walnut Raisin Cookies (page 158). (Prep time: about 30 minutes)
- Blend up some Vanilla Cashew–Hemp Milk (page 59) or your favorite nut/seed milk. (Prep time: 5 minutes)
- Wash and store produce properly so it stays fresh for a few days. Chop up some carrot sticks, bell pepper strips, and celery sticks; peel a few garlic cloves; and dice some onions. (Prep time: about 15 minutes)

Approximate total prep time: 2 hours

➤ TIMESAVERS

Most of us live very busy lives so sometimes shortcuts are in order, especially if they help us stick to a healthy eating plan. Here are a few timesavers if you're in a pinch.

Prepackaged greens:
- Organic, triple–washed greens are a huge timesaver. Get a bag each of kale, spinach, and spring/mesclun mix.

Shredded carrots:
- Make sure these are organic, if possible.

Precut fruits and vegetables:
- Cubed cantaloupe, pineapple spears, diced onions, and sliced carrot sticks are great timesavers. If possible, make sure these are organic, and not canned.

Frozen fruit:
- Keep a few bags of organic berries, mango, pineapple, and cherries in the freezer so you can whip up a quick smoothie anytime.

Boxed almond milk:
- Unsweetened and organic boxed almond milk is not nearly as good as the homemade stuff, but it's a good backup to keep on hand in case you run out of nuts.

Ginger juice:
- You can find ginger juice at many health food stores in the Asian foods section. One tablespoon of juice is equivalent to a tablespoon of grated ginger. Make sure you shake the bottle very well before using.

Premade guacamole and salsa:
- Again, these prepackaged versions are not as good as having food freshly made by loving hands, but they are convenient if you need a quick snack.

3 THE RAW & SIMPLE RECIPES

CHAPTER THREE

Tips on Following Recipes

➤ Read recipes in their entirety before starting. I have listed ingredients that need to be prepared in advance at the top of each recipe.

➤ Whenever I try new recipes, I like to follow the instructions the author's way first. Then I make notes and modify it to suit my tastes for next time.

➤ Most recipes have smaller yields, because I developed them for just my husband and myself (and we're light eaters). If you're preparing food for a family or want to make enough for a couple days, then definitely double the recipe. Just don't double the salt content. Sometimes you only need 50 percent more.

➤ Because fruits and vegetables vary in flavor and size from season to season, I've listed some ingredients with a measurement range. For example, you might see 2–4 tablespoons (30–59 ml) lemon juice or 1–2 cloves garlic. Always start with less and build your way up so you don't over-season your dish.

➤ Adjust ingredients as needed. I try to use the least amount of salt and sweetener needed, so feel free to add more (or less) if you like. Same goes for olive oil, lemon juice, and other flavorings. For some recipes, I've listed "sweeten or salt to taste," so use your discretion.

➤ Substitute ingredients as needed. Maybe you're having cashew overload. Then go ahead and use almonds or macadamia nuts instead. Or maybe you need a break from nuts all together, so try sunflower or pumpkin seeds. The flavor of the dish will change, but you might love it even more. Same goes for green leafy vegetables, sweeteners, herbs, and other seasonings.

➤ I've included some variations in many of the recipes. Have fun experimenting and adapting these recipes for yourself and your family.

Breakfast

STONE FRUIT SALAD WITH SWEET ALMOND RICOTTA

HONEY, MINT, AND CITRUS FLAVORS DRESS THIS LOVELY SEASONAL FRUIT SALAD. WONDERFULLY PAIRED WITH SWEET ALMOND RICOTTA, THIS IS THE STUFF BREAKFAST DREAMS ARE MADE OF.

MAKES 2–4 SERVINGS

PLAN AHEAD: MAKE ONE BATCH OF SWEET ALMOND RICOTTA (PAGE 147)

PREP TIME: 15 MINUTES

DRESSING

2 tablespoons (40 g) honey or agave
2 tablespoons (30 ml) olive oil
½ tablespoon (7.5 ml) lemon juice
½ tablespoon (9 ml) orange juice
1 teaspoon apple cider vinegar

SALAD

1 peach
1 plum
½ cup (78 g) cherries, sliced and pitted
2 apricots, sliced and pitted
1 batch Sweet Almond Ricotta (page 147)
¼ cup (19 g) chopped almonds
¼ cup (6 g) shredded mint

➤ Whisk together the dressing ingredients in a small bowl. Arrange the sliced peaches, plums, cherries, and apricots on a plate or in a bowl and drizzle with dressing. Place a small scoop of almond ricotta on top and garnish with chopped mint and almonds.

MORNING SCRAMBLE

. . . .

IF YOU PREFER A SAVORY BREAKFAST, THIS IS AS CLOSE TO AN EGG–TOFU SCRAMBLE AS YOU'RE GOING TO GET USING ONLY RAW INGREDIENTS AND NO HEAT. GET YOUR HANDS ON SOME BLACK SALT (WHICH ACTUALLY LOOKS PINK WHEN IT'S GROUND) IF YOU CAN. IT HAS A HIGH SULFUR CONTENT, GIVING THE AVOCADO AN EGG–LIKE QUALITY. IT'S ALSO A FUN SEASONING TO HAVE IN YOUR PANTRY TO USE IN ETHNIC SAUCES AND CHUTNEYS, ESPECIALLY INDIAN FOOD.

. . . .

MAKES 2 SERVINGS

PREP TIME: 15 MINUTES

MARINATED VEGETABLES

1 cup (70 g) sliced shiitake mushrooms
1 cup (30 g) roughly chopped spinach
1 tablespoon (15 ml) tamari
½ tablespoon (7.5 ml) olive oil
1 teaspoon finely chopped sweet onions

➤ Put all ingredients in a mason jar with a lid and shake vigorously. Let sit for five to ten minutes while you prep the scramble.

SCRAMBLE

1 large avocado
⅛–¼ teaspoon turmeric (optional)
Black or sea salt to taste
1 Roma tomato, seeded and diced

➤ Mash the avocado with the turmeric and salt. Top with marinated vegetables and diced tomatoes and serve.

CHERRY–HEMP MUESLI

THIS IS A SIMPLE EUROPEAN–INSPIRED BREAKFAST CEREAL THAT IS EASY TO MAKE AND CONVENIENT TO KEEP ON HAND FOR A QUICK BREAKFAST. IT'S ESPECIALLY GREAT TO TAKE WITH YOU WHEN TRAVELING. I FIND THE DATES BALANCE OUT THE TARTNESS OF THE CHERRIES QUITE NICELY, BUT YOU CAN SUBSTITUTE EITHER WITH YOUR FAVORITE DRIED FRUITS, SUCH AS APRICOTS, APPLES, AND CRANBERRIES. SERVE WITH CHOPPED BANANAS, APPLES, OR FRESH BERRIES AND YOUR FAVORITE NUT MILK (PAGE 59).

MAKES 6 SERVINGS

PREP TIME: 10 MINUTES

¼ **cup (56 g) dried cherries**
¼ **cup (44 g) Medjool dates**
½ **cup (75 g) almonds**
½ **teaspoon ground vanilla powder**
1 **cup (30 g) (100 g) rolled oats**
½ **cup (115 g) hemp seeds**

➤ Place the dried cherries and dates in a food processor and process until broken down into smaller pieces. Don't process for too long, though; you don't want to make a paste. Drier dates are preferred here instead of the soft, gooey ones.

➤ Add almonds and vanilla and pulse until all ingredients are incorporated but still a little chunky.

➤ Transfer the mixture to a bowl and add in oats and hemp seeds. Store in an airtight container for four weeks or longer in the refrigerator.

COOKED VARIATION: Mix with cooked quinoa and sweetened almond milk. Quinoa is an alkaline, gluten–free seed grain and is a good source of protein and B vitamins.

BANANA WALNUT OATMEAL

THIS IS MY BREAKFAST OF CHOICE WHEN I NEED SOME COMFORT FOOD. IF BANANAS ARE TOO SWEET AND STARCHY FOR YOU, LIGHTEN THIS RECIPE UP BY REPLACING THEM WITH TWO LARGE APPLES.

MAKES 2 TO 4 SERVINGS

PLAN AHEAD: MAKE ONE BATCH OF UNSWEETENED ALMOND OR CASHEW NUT MILK (SEE PAGE 59). ALSO SOAK THE OAT GROATS THE NIGHT BEFORE.

PREP TIME: 15 MINUTES

1⅓ cup (200 g) whole oat groats, soaked for 12 hours and rinsed and drained well (should yield 2 cups (300 g) soaked oat groats)
2 small bananas
1 teaspoon cinnamon
½ teaspoon vanilla extract
Pinch salt
½ cup (118 ml) unsweetened Almond or
    Cashew Milk (page 59)
½ cup (113 g) sliced bananas for garnish
⅓ cup (42 g) chopped walnuts
Maple syrup (optional)

➤ Place oat groats, bananas, cinnamon, vanilla extract, salt, and a splash of nut milk in a food processor and process until desired consistency.

NOTE: I prefer it chunky instead of smooth. It has less effect on my blood sugar and keeps me feeling fuller longer.

➤ Divide the mixture into serving bowls and add another splash or two of nut milk and stir. Top with banana slices, chopped walnuts, and additional cinnamon and drizzle with maple syrup if desired.

CHEF TIP: Make it warm by carefully heating oatmeal on the stovetop with nut milk. It will get starchy very quickly, so keep an eye on it. If you have a dehydrator, warm oatmeal for one hour at 145° F (62.8° C).

HEALTH NOTE: For centuries people have soaked their grains before eating them to remove enzyme inhibitors and phytic acid that block nutrient absorption of essential minerals such as zinc, calcium, magnesium, and iron. Some commercial oats may have a trace amount of gluten, so if you're sensitive to it make sure you only use certified gluten free oats.

Chia Pudding, Three Ways

CHIA SEEDS ARE NUTRITIOUS AND VERSATILE LITTLE SEEDS. THEY'RE A GREAT SOURCE OF OMEGA–3 AND –6 ESSENTIAL FATTY ACIDS AS WELL AS FIBER AND PROTEIN. I LOVE USING CHIA SEEDS TO MAKE A TAPIOCA–LIKE PUDDING THAT I CAN EAT FOR BREAKFAST OR DESSERT. IT'S VERY HYDRATING AND GREAT FOR MAINTAINING BLOOD SUGAR—AND I EVEN MADE IT LOW SUGAR BY USING XYLITOL.

CARDAMOM RAISIN CHIA PUDDING

THIS RECIPE IS EVERYONE'S FAVORITE, SO IF YOU'RE NEW TO CHIA PUDDING YOU MIGHT WANT TO START HERE.

MAKES 2 SERVINGS

PLAN AHEAD: MAKE ONE BATCH OF UNSWEETENED ALMOND OR CASHEW MILK (PAGE 59)

PREP TIME: 15 MINUTES, PLUS SOAKING FOR 2 HOURS TO OVERNIGHT

1 cup (235 ml) Almond or Cashew Milk (page 59)
3 tablespoons (43 g) chia seeds
2–3 tablespoons (30–45 ml) xylitol or 2 tablespoons (28 g) agave
½ teaspoon cinnamon
¼–½ teaspoon cardamom
2 tablespoons (28 g) raisins
¼ cup (31 g) chopped walnuts (optional)

➤ Combine the nut milk with all ingredients except walnuts and mix well. Let the mixture rest for ten minutes and stir again until thoroughly combined. Put the mixture in the refrigerator for a couple hours or overnight for the chia seeds to fully absorb the flavors. When set, add more nut milk or chia seeds if needed, then top with walnuts and serve. This pudding will last two to three days in the refrigerator if stored in an airtight container.

SUPERFOOD CHIA PUDDING

EAT SUPERFOODS FOR A SUPER DAY! GO AHEAD AND PLAY AROUND WITH OTHER SUPERFOODS SUCH AS LUCUMA, MESQUITE, MACA, MULBERRIES, OR GOLDENBERRIES TO MAKE YOUR OWN PERFECT PUDDING.

MAKES 2 SERVINGS

PLAN AHEAD: MAKE ONE BATCH OF UNSWEETENED ALMOND OR CASHEW MILK (PAGE 59)

PREP TIME: 15 MINUTES, PLUS SOAKING FOR 2 HOURS TO OVERNIGHT

1 cup (235 ml) unsweetened Almond or Cashew Milk (page 59)
3 tablespoons (43 g) chia seeds
2–3 tablespoons (30–45 ml) xylitol or 2 tablespoons (28 g) agave
2 tablespoons (28 g) hemp seeds
2 tablespoons (28 g) goji berries
1 tablespoon (15 g) shredded coconut
1 tablespoon (15 g) cacao nibs

➤ Combine all ingredients and mix well. Let the mixture rest for ten minutes and stir again until thoroughly combined. Place the mixture in the refrigerator for a couple hours or overnight so the chia seeds can fully absorb the flavors. When set, add more nut milk or chia seeds if needed. The pudding will last two to three days in refrigerator stored in an airtight container.

HAZELNUT CHOCOLATE CHIA PUDDING

CHOCOLATE FOR BREAKFAST? *AND* IT TASTES LIKE MY FAVORITE ITALIAN HAZELNUT CHOCOLATE SPREAD? HECK, YEAH! MAKE THIS THE NIGHT BEFORE SO IT'S READY WHEN YOU WAKE UP OR SAVE IT FOR DESSERT LATER.

MAKES 2 SERVINGS

PREP TIME: 15 MINUTES, PLUS SOAKING TIME FOR 2 HOURS TO OVERNIGHT

1 cup (30 g) (235 ml) water
¼ cup (38 g) hazelnuts
3 tablespoons (43 g) chia seeds
3 tablespoons (30–45 ml) xylitol
   or 2½ tablespoons (38 ml) agave nectar
1½ (22.5 g) tablespoons cacao powder
1 (7 g) tablespoon chopped hazelnuts
1 small banana, sliced

➤ Process water and hazelnuts in a blender and strain the liquid through a nut milk bag (see page 27). Whisk together the strained hazelnut milk and the chia seeds, sweetener, and cacao powder in a bowl. Let the mixture rest for ten minutes and stir again until thoroughly combined.

➤ Place the mixture in the refrigerator overnight so the chia seeds can fully absorb the flavors. Serve with chopped hazelnuts and sliced bananas. This pudding will last three days in the refrigerator stored in an airtight container.

CHEF TIP: Unlike other nuts, hazelnuts do not need to be soaked because they do not contain enzyme inhibitors like almonds do.

Smoothies

APPLE PIE SMOOTHIE

THIS IS A FUN AND COMFORTING WAY TO START THE DAY, ESPECIALLY IN THE FALL WHEN CRISP, SWEET APPLES COME INTO SEASON. I PREFER MY SMOOTHIE ROOM TEMPERATURE AND TOPPED OFF WITH A SPRINKLE OF CHERRY HEMP MUESLI (PAGE 44). APPLES VARY FROM VERY SWEET TO VERY TART, SO ADJUST THE AMOUNT OF LEMON JUICE YOU USE AND ADD A LITTLE SWEETENER IF NEEDED.

MAKES 2 SERVINGS

PLAN AHEAD: MAKE UNSWEETENED ALMOND OR CASHEW MILK (PAGE 59)

PREP TIME: 15 MINUTES

1½ cups (353 ml) unsweetened Almond
  or Cashew Milk (page 59)
3 large Red Delicious or your favorite apples, chopped
1 teaspoon pumpkin pie spice
2–4 tablespoons (30–59 ml) lemon juice
3 tablespoons (15 g) ground chia seeds
2 teaspoons vanilla extract or ½ vanilla bean, scraped
Sweeten to taste
Cinnamon for garnish

➤ Put all of the ingredients in a blender and blend until smooth. Top with a sprinkling of cinnamon, then allow it to sit for five minutes to thicken.

CHEF TIP: Make it green! Throw in a handful of spinach or other leafy greens to give it an extra nutrient boost.

HEALTH NOTE: Finnish researchers found that regular apple eaters had fewer strokes than people who did not eat apples. Besides being high in fiber and antioxidants, apples can help regulate blood sugar and lower bad LDL cholesterol, and they contain loads of pectin, which helps reduce belly fat and pull unwanted toxins from the colon.

PUMPKIN SMOOTHIE

I WASN'T SURE WHAT TO DO WITH MY DECORATIVE AUTUMN PUMPKINS AFTER THE HOLIDAYS WERE OVER. I WAS PLEASANTLY SURPRISED TO FIND THAT RAW PUMPKIN COULD TASTE THIS GOOD!

MAKES 2 SERVINGS

PLAN AHEAD: 1 BATCH OF ALMOND MILK (PAGE 59)

PREP TIME: 15 MINUTES

1 cup (235 ml) Almond Milk (page 59)
2 cups (300 g) fresh grated pumpkin
1¼ teaspoons pumpkin pie spice
6 Medjool dates, pitted
¼ vanilla bean, scraped, or 1 teaspoon vanilla extract
4 ice cubes
Dash of sea salt

➤ Put all ingredients into a blender and blend until smooth. Adjust flavorings as needed. If the mixture is too thick, add more almond milk.

HAPPY MONKEY

THIS THICK AND HEARTY SMOOTHIE IS MY HUSBAND'S SIGNATURE "DA KINE" PRE-SURF BREAKFAST. IT WILL DEFINITELY FILL YOU UP AND PUT A HAPPY SPRING IN YOUR STEP ALL MORNING.

MAKES 2 SERVINGS

PLAN AHEAD: MAKE A BATCH OF YOUR FAVORITE NUT MILK (PAGE 59) AND SLICE AND FREEZE BANANA CHUNKS THE NIGHT BEFORE.

PREP TIME: 10 MINUTES

1½ cups (353 ml) Almond or Cashew milk (pg. 59)
2 cups (300 g) frozen banana chunks
½ cup (40 g) shredded coconut
3 tablespoons (42 g) cacao nibs
3 tablespoons (42 g) cacao powder
2 tablespoons (28 g) raw almond butter
Sweeten to taste

➤ Put all ingredients into a blender, process, and serve immediately. Add more nut milk to achieve desired consistency.

CHEF TIP: Upgrade this smoothie by adding your favorite protein powder or superfood such as maca, tocotrienals, reishi, or chaga mushroom.

Green Smoothies

A big thanks to Victoria Boutenko and her raw family for introducing green smoothies to the mainstream. She discovered that blended greens are easier to digest and assimilate than greens chewed with our teeth. The blades of a high-power blender can break the tough cellular wall and release the chlorophyll, minerals, and other nutrients so they can quickly enter our bloodstream. Green smoothies can be fruit- or vegetable-based with a hefty amount of green leafy vegetables like spinach, kale, Swiss chard, romaine, green and red leaf lettuce, arugula, and lambsquarters to name a few. Any smoothie in this book can be made green without sacrificing too much of the flavor. Sweet fruit and acids like lemon and lime juice help balance the bitterness of some of greens. Ease into it with some spinach and then try some heartier, dark greens. Greens are very good in fruit smoothies to help balance blood sugar because they add extra fiber and minerals to keep our glycemic load low and slow the absorption of the sugars For green smoothie recipes, check out my first book, *Going Raw*, as well as Victoria Boutenko's books *Green for Life* and *Green Smoothie Revolution*.

GARDEN SMOOTHIE

YOU CAN JAZZ UP THE FLAVOR WITH A FEW SPRIGS OF BASIL, CILANTRO, PARSLEY, OR DILL FROM YOUR GARDEN OR A SMALL PIECE OF SERRANO PEPPER OR DASH OF CAYENNE FOR MORE KICK. IN THE WARMER MONTHS, I THROW IN A FEW ICE CUBES FOR A TRULY REFRESHING DRINK.

MAKES 2 SERVINGS

PREP TIME: 15 MINUTES

1 cup (255 ml) water
1 cup (30 g) spinach or kale
1 tomato, chopped
1 red bell pepper, seeded and chopped
½ cucumber, chooped
1 stalk celery, chopped
juice of ½ lemon
1 small clove garlic
½ avocado
a few sprigs of your favorite herbs
salt to taste

➤ Place all ingredients in a blender and process until smooth. Adjust seasonings as needed and serve immediately.

TROPICO GELATO

HERE'S A LUXURIOUS SMOOTHIE YOU CAN EAT WITH A SPOON. I NOTICED A LOT OF THE RESTAURANTS IN SANTA TERESA, COSTA RICA, SERVE THEIR SMOOTHIES THIS WAY SO I STARTED MAKING THEM AT HOME. YOU'LL HAVE BETTER RESULTS WITH A HIGH-POWER BLENDER LIKE A VITAMIX WHERE YOU CAN USE A PLUNGER TO KEEP THINGS MOVING.

MAKES 2 SERVINGS

PLAN AHEAD: MAKE COCONUT MILK (PAGE 29) AND FREEZE FRUIT

PREP TIME: 10 MINUTES

½ cup (118 ml) Coconut Milk (page 29)
1 cup (175 g) fresh or frozen mango, thawed
1 cup (150 g) frozen banana chunks
1 cup (159 g) frozen pineapple chunks

➤ Place all ingredients in a blender and blend until smooth, but still thick and icy. Serve immediately.

CHERRY-CACAO SMOOTHIE

MY TASTE TESTERS LIKEN THIS ONE TO A VERY POPULAR ICE CREAM FLAVOR NAMED AFTER THE LATE GRATEFUL DEAD SINGER. PERSONALLY, I THINK IT TASTES LIKE HEAVEN.

MAKES 2 SERVINGS

PLAN AHEAD: MAKE ALMOND OR CASHEW MILK (PG 59)

PREP TIME: 10 MINUTES

2 cups (310 g) fresh or frozen cherries,
    pitted and thawed
½ cup (120 g) young Thai coconut meat
½ cup (118 ml) Almond or Cashew Milk (page 59)
1 ½ tablespoons (22.5 g) cacao nibs
½ tablespoon (7.5 g) vanilla extract
    or ½ vanilla bean, scraped
Dash of sea salt
4 or more ice cubes
Several drops stevia or sweetener of choice

➤ Put all of the ingredients into a blender and blend until smooth.

HEALTH NOTE: Cherries contain nineteen times more beta carotene than strawberries and blueberries, have powerful antiinflammatory properties, and even contain a significant amount of natural melatonin, a hormone formed in the pineal gland that helps regulate sleep.

Clockwise:
Tropio Gelato, Cherry-Cacao Smoothie,
Super Antioxidant Coco-Berry Smoothie (page 56),
and Orange Bee Love (page 56).

ORANGE BEE LOVE

THIS LIGHT AND FROTHY ORANGE SMOOTHIE CONTAINS SOME OF NATURE'S PERFECT FOOD. I RECOMMEND USING ORANGE BLOSSOM HONEY IN THIS RECIPE IF YOU CAN FIND IT. IT'S A VERY FRAGRANT VARIETY THAT GIVES THIS BEVERAGE A LOVELY DIMENSION.

MAKES 2 TO 3 SERVINGS

PREP TIME: 15 MINUTES

3 oranges, peeled and chopped
¼ cantaloupe, chopped
1 tablespoon (15 g) bee pollen
½ tablespoon (7.5 g) vanilla extract
½ tablespoon (10 g) raw honey or to taste
4 ice cubes

➤ Put all ingredients in a blender and blend until smooth.

HEALTH NOTE: Honey has antimicrobial, antifungal, and antiviral properties, while bee pollen contains almost a hundred essential vitamins, minerals, enzymes, and amino acids that have immune–boosting, cholesterol–lowering, and anticancer properties. Make sure you buy high–quality (raw/unfiltered) products from an ethical source, but steer clear if you have a bee allergy!

SUPER ANTIOXIDANT COCO–BERRY SMOOTHIE

I LIKE TO LOAD UP THIS CREAMY BERRY SMOOTHIE WITH SOME TASTY BUT LESSER KNOWN SUPERFOODS LIKE TOCOTRIENOLS, MESQUITE, AND LUCUMA (SEE BELOW). DON'T WORRY IF THEY ARE NOT SOLD WHERE YOU LIVE. THIS SMOOTHIE IS STILL GREAT WITHOUT THEM.

MAKES 2 SERVINGS

PLAN AHEAD: MAKE 1 CUP (235 ML) COCONUT MILK (PAGE 29) AND BASIC NUT MILK (PAGE 59)

PREP TIME: 10 MINUTES

2 cups (300 g) frozen mixed berries
1 cup (235 ml) Coconut Milk (page 29)
½ cup (118 ml) Basic Nut Milk (page 59) or water
1–2 tablespoons (15–28 g) xylitol or sweetener of choice
½ tablespoon (7.5 g) vanilla extract or dash of
    vanilla powder
2 tablespoons (28 g) tocotrienol powder (optional)
1 tablespoon (15 g) mesquite (optional)
½ tablespoon (7.5 g) lucuma (optional)

➤ Blend all ingredients in a blender until smooth.

HEALTH NOTE: Tocotrienol powder is a delicious whole–food supplement made from rice bran and is very high in vitamin E, a powerful antioxidant. It also contains additional antioxidants like selenium, CoQ_{10}, glutathione, as well as B vitamins, essential fatty acids, and minerals. Add it to smoothies and desserts for a nutritional boost.

MESQUITE POWDER: For ages, Native Americans have consumed and prized these edible pods from the Mesquite tree. It is dried and ground into flour that is sweet and smoky with a hint of caramel. It can be used to sweeten smoothies and desserts and can even be used as a flour substitute in many recipes. It's low glycemic, high in fiber, and a good source of lysine, calcium, iron, manganese, zinc, and potassium.

LUCUMA POWDER: The fruit of the lucuma tree has been an Incan superfood for thousands of years. The pulp is dried and ground into a fine flour that has a unique sweetness with a hint of maple that can be added to smoothies, ice cream, and other desserts. It's low glycemic and contains iron, calcium, protein, fiber, and an array of trace minerals.

HAZELNUT FIG SHAKE

THIS FANTASTICALLY DELICIOUS SMOOTHIE WAS INSPIRED BY ONE OFFERED AT MY FAVORITE LA RAW EATERY, CAFÉ GRATITUDE.

MAKES 2 SERVINGS

PLAN AHEAD: FREEZE 1 ½ CUPS (225 G) BANANA CHUNKS.

PREP TIME: 10 MINUTES

2 cups (235 ml) water
½ cup (88 g) hazelnuts
6 small dried figs
1½ cups (225 g) frozen banana chunks
½ vanilla bean, scraped
Dash sea salt

➤ Put water and hazelnuts in a blender until the nuts are broken down. Strain the liquid through a nut milk bag, and then return hazelnut milk to the blender and add the remaining ingredients. Blend until smooth and serve immediately.

Beverages

BASIC NUT MILK

MAKING YOUR OWN NUT MILK IS EASIER THAN IT SOUNDS. ONCE YOU'VE TRIED IT, YOU'LL NEVER WANT TO GO BACK TO THE BOXED STUFF AGAIN.

SOAK TIME: 2–12 HOURS

PREP TIME: 5 MINUTES

**1 cup nuts (220 g), soaked and drained
(see Soaking Nuts & Seeds on page 28)**

4 cups (940 ml) water

➤ Blend nuts and water in a blender.

➤ Strain pulp through a nut milk bag.

➤ Sweeten to taste, if desired

➤ Store in an airtight container in the refrigerator for 3–4 days.

➤ Shake before using.

CHEF TIP: The leftover nut pulp can be dehydrated and then ground into a fine flour to use for desserts. Flour will last several months in an airtight container in the refrigerator. If you don't have a dehydrator you can always add it to your compost.

VANILLA CASHEW HEMP MILK

HEMP SEEDS HAVE A VERY EARTHY FLAVOR THAT I LIKE TO BALANCE OUT WITH THE CASHEWS, VANILLA, AND SWEETENER. THE GREAT THING ABOUT USING CASHEWS AND HEMP SEEDS IS THAT THERE IS VERY LITTLE TO NO PULP LEFT AFTER BLENDING. NO NEED TO STRAIN WITH A NUT MILK BAG UNLESS YOU WANT A LIGHTER MILK.

PREP TIME: 5 MINUTES

MAKES 4 CUPS.

**½ cup (110 g) cashews
½ cup (110 g) hemp seeds
4 cups (940 ml) water
¼ teaspoon liquid stevia or sweetener of choice
½ vanilla bean, scraped or 1 tablespoon vanilla extract
⅛ teaspoon sea salt (optional)**

➤ Place all ingredients in a blender and process until smooth.

➤ Store in an airtight container in the refrigerator for 3–4 days.

➤ Shake before using.

HEALTHY MARY

I WAS ON THE HUNT FOR THE PERFECT BLOODY MARY UNTIL I LEARNED THE BEST WERE MADE WITH CLAM JUICE AND BEEF BOUILLON. NOW I MAKE MY OWN WITH FRESH TOMATOES AND BOLD SEASONINGS. THEY DON'T CALL IT THE WORLD'S MOST COMPLEX COCKTAIL FOR NOTHING, SO ADJUST IT TO SUIT YOUR TASTES—AND IF YOU WANT TO ADD A SPLASH OF ORGANIC VODKA, I WON'T TELL.

MAKES 2 SERVINGS

PREP TIME: 15 MINUTES

3 cups (540 g) chopped tomatoes
1 cup (235 ml) water
⅓ cup (50 g) chopped red bell pepper
1 ½ tablespoons (22.5 g) fresh grated horseradish root
1 jalapeno, seeded
1 small clove garlic
1 teaspoon tamarind paste
¼ teaspoon celery seed
¼ teaspoon sea salt or to taste
Cayenne and fresh ground pepper to taste
Celery stalk and lime wedge for garnish

➤ Put all of the ingredients into blender and blend until smooth. Adjust seasonings to taste and serve immediately over ice. Garnish with the celery and lime wedge.

CHEF TIP: Add a handful of spinach to make it a Green Mary!

COCOJITO

I CAN'T GET ENOUGH OF THIS COCONUT, LIME, AND MINT SLUSHY. IT'S THE PERFECT FROZEN DELIGHT ON A HOT SUMMER DAY.

MAKES 2–3 SERVINGS

PLAN AHEAD: MAKE 1 CUP (235 ML) COCONUT MILK (PAGE 29)

PREP TIME: 10 MINUTES

4 cups (512 g) ice
2 limes, rind removed
1 cup (235 ml) Coconut Milk (page 29)
⅓ cup (100 g) agave or sweetener of choice
⅓ cup (8 g) mint leaves

➤ Blend all ingredients in a blender until smooth. Pour into glasses and garnish with mint leaves or lime wedge. Serve immediately.

STRAWBERRY DAIQUIRI

BECAUSE OF THE FERMENTED WATER KEFIR, THIS ACTUALLY TASTES LIKE AN ALCOHOLIC BEVERAGE. THIS MAKES A GREAT DRINK TO SERVE AT PARTIES, AND IS A DELICIOUS SUMMER CLEANSER.

MAKES 3–4 SERVINGS

PLAN AHEAD: YOU WILL NEED A BATCH OF BASIC OR FRUITY WATER KEFIR FOR THIS RECIPE (PAGE 136).

PREP TIME: 10 MINUTES

1½ cups (255 g) chopped strawberries
1½ cups (353 ml) Basic or Fruity Water Kefir (page 136)
3 tablespoons (44 ml) lime juice
Few drops stevia or favorite sweetener to taste
3 cups of ice

➤ Blend all ingredients in a blender and serve immediately.

WATERMELON–FENNEL–MINT CHILLER

THIS IS HANDS DOWN MY FAVORITE SUMMER BEVERAGE, AS WELL AS A GREAT DETOX DRINK. I PRACTICALLY LIVE ON THIS WHEN WATERMELON SEASON COMES AROUND. THE FENNEL AND MINT ARE VERY COOLING AND HELP TO BALANCE OUT THE SWEETNESS OF THE WATERMELON.

MAKES 2 SERVINGS

PREP TIME: 10 MINUTES

4 cups (600 g) cubed watermelon
1 cup (150 g) chopped fennel, white bulb only
⅓ cup (8 g) loosely packed fresh mint
6 ice cubes
Sweeten to taste, if needed

➤ Place all ingredients in a blender and process till frothy. Serve immediately.

HEALTH NOTE: Watermelons contain more lycopene than tomatoes. They are also an excellent source of vitamin C and beta carotene and can help improve kidney function.

Cleansing Drinks and Mocktails

THESE MOCKTAILS ARE A FUN ADDITION TO A JUICE CLEANSE, PARTY, OR PICNIC, OR FOR ANY TIME YOU FEEL LIKE SOMETHING OUT OF THE ORDINARY. ALL OF THESE BEVERAGES CAN BE MADE IN THE BLENDER AND WILL YIELD AROUND 16 OUNCES (475 ML). A CITRUS REAMER AND NUT MILK BAG ARE ALSO VERY HELPFUL FOR SOME OF THE RECIPES.

INDIAN-SPICED ORANGE

1½ cup (354 ml) fresh–squeezed orange juice
½ cup (118 ml) Almond or Cashew Milk (page 59)
¼ teaspoon garam masala

➤ Put all the ingredients in a blender and process. Serve over ice.

MILK AND HONEY REFRESHER

1½ cup (338 g) grapefruit (about 3 small), peeled, remove pith
¾ cup (176 ml) Almond Milk (page 59)
1–2 tablespoons (20–40 g) honey

➤ Put ingredients in a blender and process. Serve over ice.

SPARKLING GRAPEFRUIT

1 cup (236 ml) freshly squeezed grapefruit juice
1 cup (235 ml) sparkling mineral water
Few drops stevia

➤ Put all ingredients in a blender and process. Serve over ice.

GREEN JUICE MOCKTAIL

3 cups (510 g) chopped honeydew or cantaloupe
½ cup (15 g) spinach
½-inch piece fresh ginger
½ cup (118 ml) or more sparkling water
Stevia to taste

➤ Put the melon, spinach, and ginger in a blender and process until smooth. Strain the liquid through a nut milk bag. Pour the juice into a small pitcher and add sparkling water. Serve over ice.

VEGGIES ON THE ROCKS

2 cups (300 g) chopped red bell pepper
1½ cups (150 g) chopped celery
¾ cup (176 ml) water
⅓ cup (47 g) sauerkraut with juice
Dash of cayenne (optional)

➤ Put all ingredients except the cayenne into a blender and blend. Strain the liquid through a nut milk bag. Add additional sauerkraut juice if you like it more tart. Serve over ice with a dash of cayenne.

LEMON-LIME CHIA FRESCA

2 cups (470 ml) sparkling mineral water or filtered water
2 tablespoons (30 ml) lemon juice
2 tablespoons (30 ml) lime juice
1 tablespoon (15 g) chia seeds
1 tablespoon (6 g) chopped mint
Few drops stevia or sweetener of choice

➤ Mix all ingredients in a large glass or small pitcher. Let sit for ten minutes and then stir again. Serve over ice.

GRAPE CHIA FRESCA

1 cup (150 g) red grapes
1 cup (235 ml) Basic or Fruity Water Kefir (page 136) or sparkling mineral water
1 tablespoon (15 g) chia seeds

➤ Put the grapes and kefir into a blender and process until smooth. Pour the liquid into a glass or small pitcher. Add chia seeds and stir. Let sit for ten minutes and then stir again. Serve over ice.

Juices

JUICING IS A GREAT WAY TO GET AN ABUNDANT AMOUNT OF VITAMINS AND MINERALS IN ONE GLASS. IT'S MUCH EASIER TO DRINK A BIG SALAD THAN TO SPEND 30–40 MINUTES CHEWING IT UP, PLUS THE NUTRIENTS ARE EASER TO ASSIMILATE AS THE CELL WALLS OF THE PLANT ARE BROKEN DOWN MORE EFFICIENTLY IN THE JUICING PROCESS. VITAMINS, MINERALS, AND CHLOROPHYLL INSTANTLY ENTER THE BLOOD STREAM THROUGH THE STOMACH, OXYGENATE YOUR BLOOD, AND ENERGIZE YOUR BRAIN. MAKE GREEN JUICES YOUR NEW MORNING CUP OF JOE AND FEEL THE DIFFERENCE!

I find cucumbers and celery make a great base for juices. I especially like cucumbers in fruit juices because they're somewhat neutral and help to water down overly sweet fruit juice. Pretty much any produce can be juiced (except avocados and bananas). Play around with ingredients, especially the greens. Dive into some chard, arugula, collards, watercress, broccoli, sprouts, etc. for some unique flavor combinations.

For tips on juice fasting see page 15.

RED DELISH LEMONADE

4 red delicious apples
2 Myer lemons, peeled
2 cucumbers

MAROON 5

1 beet with green tops
1 green apple
1 cucumber
½ lemon
2–inch piece of ginger

GREEN DAY

1 cucumber
4 stalks celery
1 cup (30 g) spinach
1 cup (60 g) parsley
1 lime
1 red or green apple
small handful mint

KING CRIMSON

1 pound (455 g) carrots
2–3 Roma tomatoes
2 red bell peppers

SUCCO DI POMODORO

3 Roma tomatoes
4 large stalks celery
2 cloves garlic
1 cup (40 g) basil
dash of cayenne

MELON COOLER

½ medium honeydew (include rind if organic)
1 cucumber
1 cup (96 g) mint

FRESH FENNEL

1 cucumber
1 bulb fennel
1 green apple
Handful spinach

NOTE: Each recipe yields around 16 ounces (475 ml)

Teas

WARM TEAS ARE A GREAT WAY TO STAY COZY DURING THE COLDER MONTHS. IF YOU'RE TRYING TO EAT RAW DURING THE WINTER, IT'S ALMOST ESSENTIAL THAT YOU DRINK WARM BEVERAGES. HERE'S THE RECIPE TO MY FAVORITE MORNING BLEND.

Few slices of dried astragalus root
2 tablespoons (28 g) goji berries
1 teaspoon gynostemma tea
½ vanilla bean, scraped
(use the leftovers from another recipe)
Few drops stevia liquid or your favorite sweetener

➤ Place all the ingredients into a quart jar and fill it with hot, not boiling, water. Let the mixture steep for ten minutes, then enjoy. You can steep this tea twice.

➤ ASTRAGALUS ROOT
A great immune–boosting herb with antiviral properties. Considered one of the great tonic herbs of Traditional Chinese Medicine, it builds energy (Qi), tonifies the lungs and spleen, and warms the body.

➤ GOJI BERRIES
An ancient tonic herb, high in antioxidants and antiaging properties, and they give this tea a little bit of sweetness.

➤ GYNOSTEMMA
A very powerful adaptogenic herb popular in Asia. It is very calming and anti–inflammatory, and has been shown to strengthen the immune system, lower cholesterol and high blood pressure, improve cardiovascular function, and regulate blood glucose levels.

There are many unique ingredients such as medicinal mushrooms, roots, and herbs you can use to make your own concoction. Visit an herbalist in your area and have them make you a tea blend based on your personal needs.

Soups, Sides & Starters

SOUTHWEST CORN CHOWDER

THIS IS A WONDERFUL WAY TO ENJOY SUMMER'S BOUNTY OF SWEET CORN. THIS HEARTY, RICH SOUP IS GREAT TO SERVE TO FAMILY AND GUESTS WHO DON'T ESPECIALLY CARE FOR THE USUAL RAW GAZPACHO SOUPS. MAKE SURE YOU ONLY USE ORGANIC CORN, THOUGH, AS THE MAJORITY OF ALL CORN PRODUCED IS GENETICALLY MODIFIED.

MAKES 4 SERVINGS

PREP TIME: 20 MINUTES

SOUP BASE

5 cups (875 g) fresh sweet corn kernels (about 5 ears) or frozen, thawed, 1 cup (130 g) reserved
2 cups (470 ml) water
¼ avocado
3 cloves garlic
¼ cup (59 ml) lime juice
1½ teaspoon sea salt
½ teaspoon chipotle powder
¼ teaspoon black pepper

ADD-INS

1 tomato, diced
½ avocado, diced
¼ cup (4 g) chopped cilantro
Olive oil

➤ If using fresh corn, remove the corn kernels carefully using a knife.

➤ In a blender, blend together 4 cups (700 g) corn, water, avocado, garlic, lime juice, chipotle powder, salt, and pepper until smooth.

➤ Stir in the additional 1 cup (175 g) of corn kernels and then pour into four serving bowls and top with diced tomatoes, avocados, chopped cilantro, a drizzle of olive oil, and a dash of pepper if desired.

CHEF TIP: Warm this chowder by gently heating in a saucepan on low heat, stirring frequently, or put it in a dehydrator for one hour at 145° F (63° C).

HEALTH NOTE: Corn is high in antioxidants, potassium, and folic acid. When it's cooked, it becomes a starchy complex carbohydrate; when it is raw, it is a fibrous vegetable. Raw corn is easier to digest, has less effect on blood sugar, and won't affect the waistline.

CUCUMBER BASIL SOUP

THIS LIGHT AND CREAMY CUCUMBER SOUP CAN BE SERVED CHILLED OR AT ROOM TEMPERATURE.

MAKES 4 SERVINGS

PLAN AHEAD: SOAK THE CASHEWS IF YOU DO NOT HAVE A HIGH–POWER BLENDER.

PREP TIME: 15 MINUTES

2 cucumbers, peeled and chopped
½ cup (75 g) cashews, soaked for 2 hours
1 cup (235 ml) water
½ small serrano pepper, seeded,
   or ¼ teaspoon cayenne pepper
1 clove garlic
1 cup (30 g) fresh basil
3–4 tablespoons (44–59 ml) lemon juice
¾ teaspoon sea salt
¼ cup (6 g) chopped mint
Olive or flax seed oil to taste

➤ Process all ingredients except the mint and oil in a blender until smooth. Divide the mixture into serving bowls, top with chopped mint, and drizzle with oil. This soup will keep for two days in the refrigerator.

HEALTH NOTE: Besides its tantalizing aroma and culinary uses, basil is a prized medicinal herb. It has strong antiinflammatory and antibacterial properties and has been used for centuries to treat everything from colds, fevers, coughs, and other respiratory disorders to skin conditions, stress, toothaches, and headaches. It's most powerful in its fresh, raw form.

CARROT–GINGER COCONUT SOUP

I MADE THIS BEAUTIFUL, RICH SOUP WITH RAW CHEF EXTRAORDINAIRE MATTHEW KENNEY (WWW.MATTHEWKENNEYCUISINE.COM) FOR A PRIVATE DINNER WE HOSTED, SO I CAN'T TAKE ALL THE CREDIT FOR COMING UP WITH IT. SUBTLY SWEET, SPICY, AND, OH, SO FLAVORFUL, IT'S SURE TO BECOME A STAPLE IN YOUR HOME.

MAKES 4–6 SERVINGS

PLAN AHEAD: MAKE 2 CUPS (470 ML) OF COCONUT MILK (PAGE 29) AND 2 CUPS (470 ML) OF CARROT JUICE.

PREP TIME: 15 MINUTES

2 cups (470 ml) Coconut Milk (page 29)
2 cups (470 ml) carrot juice
¼ cup (59 ml) lime juice
2 teaspoons grated ginger or ginger juice
¼ small avocado
½ teaspoon sea salt
¼ teaspoon cayenne
Fresh black pepper to taste
Chopped cilantro for garnish

➤ Put all ingredients except cilantro into a blender and process until very smooth. Adjust seasonings as needed. Add more avocado or coconut meat if you want it thicker. This soup will keep for two days in the refrigerator.

CHEF TIP: Use organic carrot juice if you don't have a juicer or if you're short on time. To warm it, blend it for an additional minute or two, or carefully heat it in a saucepan on low.

MUSHROOM MISO SOUP

I USE TWO TYPES OF MUSHROOMS IN THIS SOUP: CRIMINI MUSHROOMS, ALSO KNOWN AS BABY PORTOBELLOS, FOR THE BASE, AND MARINATED SHIITAKE MUSHROOMS FOR THE ADD-INS. THIS GIVES THE SOUP MORE DIMENSION AND ROBUST FLAVOR.

MAKES 4 SERVINGS

PLAN AHEAD: MAKE ALMOND OR CASHEW MILK (PAGE 59)

PREP TIME: 15 MINUTES

MARINATED MUSHROOMS

2 cups (150 g) sliced shiitake mushrooms
2 tablespoons (28 g) tamari

➤ Put mushrooms and tamari in a mason jar, close the lid tightly, and shake vigorously. Let the mixture sit while you make the base.

SOUP BASE

2 cups (470 ml) Almond or Cashew Milk (page 59)
1 cup (30 g) (100 g) chopped crimini mushrooms
¼ cup (69 g) chickpea miso paste
2 tablespoons (30 ml) brown rice vinegar
1 clove garlic
1–2 tablespoon (15–30 ml) olive oil

ADD-INS

2 cups (200 g) bean sprouts
1–2 green onions, green part only, thinly sliced

➤ Blend all soup base ingredients until smooth. Divide the base between four bowls and add in the marinated mushrooms, bean sprouts, and green onions. Drizzle with additional olive oil, if you like. This soup is best eaten the day it is made.

CURRIED CAULIFLOWER SOUP

IN THE PAST, I HAVE USED COOKED CAULIFLOWER AS A REPLACEMENT FOR POTATOES AND WAS PLEASANTLY SURPRISED THAT GIVING RAW CAULIFLOWER A GOOD, LONG BLEND WITH THE COCONUT MILK GIVES THIS SOUP THE SAME BODY AND FEEL AS COOKED POTATO SOUP. I'M ALSO TOTALLY IN LOVE WITH THE COMBINATION OF COCONUT, FRAGRANT CURRY (I USE FLORAL ESSENCE CURRY FROM FRANK'S FINEST), SALTY MISO, AND SWEET MEDJOOL DATES. ALL OF IT HELPS MELLOW THE FLAVOR OF THE CAULIFLOWER TO CREATE A WONDERFUL COMFORT SOUP. THIS CAN BE WARMED GENTLY OVER THE STOVETOP AS WELL OR BLENDED FOR AN ADDITIONAL TWO OR THREE MINUTES IN A HIGH–POWER BLENDER.

PLAN AHEAD: MAKE 2 CUPS (470 ML) COCONUT MILK (PAGE 29)

PREP TIME: 10 MINUTES

2 cups (470 ml) Coconut Milk (page 29)
2 cups (590 g) chopped cauliflower
½ cup (118 ml) water
¼ cup (69 g) chickpea miso paste
3 tablespoons (44 ml) lemon juice
2–3 teaspoons (4–6 g) curry blend
2 Medjool dates, pitted

➤ Process all ingredients in a blender until smooth. Use additional water if needed, and adjust seasonings to your liking.

➤ This soup will keep for two to three days in the refrigerator.

NOTE: Cardamom pods (as seen in the photo) add a nice aromatic touch to the soup, but I don't recommend eating them!

WATERMELON AND HEIRLOOM TOMATO GAZPACHO

THIS CLEANSING COLD SOUP IS A LOVELY, SWEET AND SAVORY TWIST ON TRADITIONAL TOMATO GAZPACHO. USE COLORFUL HEIRLOOM TOMATOES IF THEY ARE IN SEASON WHERE YOU LIVE OR SUBSTITUTE WITH ROMA TOMATOES.

MAKES 3–4 SERVINGS

PREP TIME: 30 MINUTES

SOUP BASE

3 cups (450 g) chopped watermelon, including some of the inner white rind
2 tablespoons (30 ml) lime juice
1½ tablespoons (9 g) chopped fresh mint
1½ tablespoons (4 g) chopped fresh basil
1 clove garlic
½ teaspoon sea salt or to taste

ADD–INS

1 cup (30 g) (180 g) multicolored heirloom tomatoes, diced
1 cup (150 g) watermelon, diced
¾ cup (89 g) diced cucumber, peeled and seeded
⅓ cup (55 g) white onions, diced

➤ Process all ingredients for the soup base in a blender until smooth. Transfer the purée to a large bowl and add diced tomatoes, watermelon, cucumbers, and onions and stir to combine. Chill this soup for an hour or two before serving. This will keep for two days in the refrigerator.

RED BELL PEPPER HUMMUS

I HAVE ONE WORD FOR THIS: MMMMM! SERVE WITH CRUDITÉS OR CRACKERS, OR USE AS A SPREAD FOR WRAPS.

MAKES 6–8 SERVINGS

PREP TIME: 10 MINUTES

1 cup (150 g) chopped red bell pepper
½ cup (120 g) raw tahini paste
¼ cup (59 ml) lemon juice
3 tablespoons (41 g) homp seeds
3 cloves garlic
1 tablespoon (15 ml) olive oil
1 teaspoon sea salt
1 teaspoon cumin
½ teaspoon paprika
Cayenne pepper to taste

➤ Combine all the ingredients in a blender or food processor until smooth. Chill in the refrigerator to firm up. This will keep for three or four days in an airtight container in the refrigerator.

HEALTH NOTE: Bell peppers are very high in vitamin C, B6, folic acid, carotenoids, and phytonutrients. Red bells are the only ones that contain the powerful anticancer phytonutrient lycopene.

SMOKY GUACAMOLE

THIS IS ONE OF MY FAVORITE QUICK SNACKS. IT'S GREAT WITH FLAX CRACKERS OR CELERY STICKS OR SPREAD OVER A ROMAINE LETTUCE LEAF FOR AN EASY WRAP.

MAKES 4–6 SERVINGS

2 avocados
2 Roma tomatoes, seeded and diced
1 clove garlic, minced
2 teaspoons fresh lime or lemon juice
¼ teaspoon chipotle chili powder
1 tablespoon (10 g) minced red onion
¼ teaspoon sea salt or to taste

➤ Mash the avocados with a fork and stir in remaining ingredients. Adjust seasonings as desired.

➤ To store, cover the mixture with plastic wrap so the wrap completely rests on the guacamole and no air remains. Stored this way, it will keep for two to three days in the refrigerator.

NACHO CHEESE DIP

THE KEY TO MAKING THIS DIP FABULOUS IS NOT SOAKING THE CASHEWS OR MINIMALLY SOAKING FOR 30 MINUTES IF YOU DON'T HAVE A POWERFUL BLENDER. THE SWEETNESS OF THE CASHEWS IS ESSENTIAL TO THE FLAVOR BALANCE IN THIS SUPER CREAMY, LUSCIOUS CHEESE SAUCE. SERVE AS A DIP OR SPREAD IT ON EVERYTHING.

MAKES 8 SERVINGS

PLAN AHEAD: IF YOU DO NOT OWN A HIGH POWER BLENDER, SOAK CASHEWS FOR 30 MINUTES. DO NOT OVERSOAK.

PREP TIME: 10 MINUTES

1 cup (135 g) cashews
⅓ cup (50 g) chopped red bell pepper
¼ cup (59 ml) water, if using soaked cashews, 1/3 unsoaked
2 tablespoons (28 ml) lemon juice

2 tablespoons (28 ml) nutritional yeast
1 clove garlic
½ teaspoon chili powder
½ teaspoon sea salt
⅛ teaspoon ancho chili pepper, optional

➤ Blend all ingredients in a blender until very smooth and creamy. You may need to stop and start the blender to scrape sides back into the blades. Adjust seasonings as desired.

➤ Will keep for one week in the refrigerator.

MAPLE–DIJON BRUSSELS SPROUTS

• •

WHO KNEW RAW BRUSSELS SPROUTS COULD TASTE THIS GOOD? THIS MAKES A GREAT HOLIDAY SIDE DISH AND CAN EVEN BE WARMED GENTLY IN A PAN. IF YOU WANT, YOU CAN SKIP THE ARUGULA AND USE ONLY BRUSSELS SPROUTS.

• •

MAKES 4 TO 6 SERVINGS

PREP TIME: 20 MINUTES

SALAD

4 cups (352 g) Brussels sprouts, shredded
4 cups (120 g) baby arugula
⅓ cup (42 g) chopped pecans
⅓ cup (40 g) dried cranberries (optional)

DRESSING

2 tablespoons (22 g) whole-grain Dijon mustard
2 tablespoons (30 ml) apple cider vinegar
¼ cup (59 ml) olive oil
1½ tablespoons (25 ml) maple syrup
1 clove garlic, finely minced

➤ Combine all the salad ingredients in a large bowl. Whisk all the dressing ingredients in a small bowl. Pour the dressing over the salad and toss well. The salad will last a day in the refrigerator.

HEALTH NOTE: Brussels sprouts are part of the cruciferous family, which includes kale, broccoli, cabbage, and cauliflower. They top the list for having the highest content of glucosinolate, a phytonutrient that is the catalyst for forming several powerful anticancer compounds. Brussels sprouts are also very high in vitamins K and C and may help lower cholesterol.

CAULIFLOWER COUSCOUS

I'VE ALWAYS PREFERRED COOKED CAULIFLOWER OVER RAW—UNTIL I TRIED THIS RECIPE. IT'S SO FRESH AND FLAVORFUL AND A GREAT SIDE DISH TO PAIR WITH RED BELL PEPPER HUMMUS (PAGE 85).

MAKES 4 SERVINGS

PREP TIME: 30 MINUTES

½ **large head of cauliflower**
½ **bunch parsley**
¼ **cup (6 g) fresh mint**
2 Roma tomatoes, seeded and diced
¼ **cup (25 g) black olives, chopped (botija are best if you can find them)**
¼ **cup (40 g) red onions, chopped**
¼ **cup (59 ml) lemon juice**
3 tablespoons (45 ml) olive oil
1 clove garlic, minced
½ **teaspoon sea salt**
¼ **teaspoon cumin**
⅛ **teaspoon smoked paprika**
Dash cayenne (optional)

➤ Chop the cauliflower and put it in a food processor. Pulse several times until it is broken down and resembles couscous. Transfer the cauliflower to a bowl.

➤ Put the parsley and mint into the food processor and pulse until finely chopped. Add the mixture to the cauliflower. Stir in remaining ingredients and toss well. Adjust seasonings to taste. This will keep for two or three days in the refrigerator.

HEALTH NOTE: Cauliflower is another rock star from the cruciferous family. Along with containing high amounts of vitamin C (50 percent RDA in a ½ cup (50 g)) it also contains di–indolyl–methane and indole–3–carbinol, two compounds that help the body get rid of excess estrogen. Estrogen dominance has been linked to breast cancer as well as cystic fibroids, endometriosis, and polycystic ovary syndrome.

CAULIFLOWER SMASH

THIS RECIPE IS GREAT ON ITS OWN, BUT AMAZING WITH MUSHROOM GRAVY (BELOW)

MAKES 4 SERVINGS

PREP TIME: 15 MINUTES

4 cups (400 g) chopped cauliflower florets
⅓ cup (45 g) pine nuts
1½ tablespoons (18 g) nutritional yeast
1 clove garlic
½ teaspoon sea salt
⅛–¼ teaspoon black pepper

➤ Put all ingredients into a food processor and mix until you achieve a consistency like mashed potatoes. Add more nutritional yeast and seasonings, if you want it cheesier. This will keep for four days in the refrigerator.

MUSHROOM GRAVY

THIS RICH–FLAVORED GRAVY WAS MADE TO GO OVER THE CAULIFLOWER SMASH (ABOVE), BUT IT CAN ALSO BE USED OVER RAW OR STEAMED VEGETABLES, QUINOA, OR RICE.

MAKES 4 SERVINGS

PREP TIME: 15 MINUTES

1 cup (30 g) (100 g) sliced crimini mushrooms
¼ cup (59 ml) water
2 tablespoons (32 g) chickpea miso
2 tablespoons (30 ml) olive oil
2 tablespoons (28 g) tamari
1 tablespoon (10 g) chopped onion
1 teaspoon fresh thyme
1 clove garlic
Dash black pepper

➤ Process all ingredients in a blender until smooth. Add more water if needed, one tablespoon at a time. Stir before using. This will keep for four days in the refrigerator.

HEALTH NOTE: Mushrooms actually create vitamin D when exposed to sunlight. They also contain a good amount of B vitamins, selenium, iron, phosphorus, and immune–boosting and free–radical–fighting phytonutrients.

CURRIED CARROTS

• •

THIS SIMPLE INDIAN–INSPIRED DISH CAME TO ME DURING A CARROT KICK I WAS HAVING LAST WINTER. I LOVE THE WARMING SPICES WITH THE RAISINS AND CASHEWS. SAVE TIME SHREDDING YOUR CARROTS BY USING THE SHREDDING BLADE ON YOUR FOOD PROCESSOR IF YOU HAVE ONE. OTHERWISE THIS WILL BE A GREAT LITTLE ARM WORKOUT!

• •

MAKES 4 SERVINGS

PREP TIME: 20 MINUTES

4 cups (440 g) shredded carrots
⅓ cup (48 g) raisins
⅓ cup (150 g) chopped cashews
3 tablespoons (44 ml) lemon juice
2 tablespoons (12 g) finely chopped mint
2 tablespoons (30 ml) flaxseed or olive oil
1 teaspoon turmeric
½ teaspoon cinnamon
½ teaspoon coriander
¼ teaspoon cumin
⅛ teaspoon yellow mustard
⅛ teaspoon cardamom
⅛ teaspoon cayenne (optional)
Dash each of clove, nutmeg, and black pepper
¼ teaspoon sea salt or to taste

➤ Combine all ingredients in a large bowl and serve. This will last for three days in the refrigerator, but it tastes best fresh. Spruce up the flavor with a squeeze of lemon if needed.

CHEF TIP: If you don't have all the spices listed you can make it easy on yourself by using a store–bought curry blend. Use about 1–2 teaspoons for starters and add more as needed.

HEALTH NOTE: Everyone knows carrots are great for protecting our vision, but did you know they're also good for cancer, heart disease, and stroke prevention—and creating healthy, glowing skin and helping the liver flush out toxins? Now you have even more reason to chow down on those carrots!

Salads

CALEXICO SALAD

. . . .

I HAD THE MOST AMAZING WATERCRESS SALAD AT CALEXICO RESTAURANT IN BROOKLYN. IT WAS SO GOOD I HAD TO RE–CREATE IT SOON AS I GOT HOME. I LOVE THE CRUNCHY JICAMA WITH CITRUS FLAVORS AND THE SPICINESS OF THE DRESSING. IF YOU CAN'T FIND WATERCRESS, USE MACHE, MESCLUN, OR A SPRING MIX INSTEAD.

. . . .

MAKES 4 SERVINGS

PREP TIME: 30 MINUTES

PLAN AHEAD: SOAK CASHEWS FOR 2 HOURS IF YOU DO NOT HAVE A HIGH POWER BLENDER.

DRESSING

¾ cup (113 g) cashews
¾ cup (176 ml) water
¼ cup (59 ml) lime or lemon juice
1 clove garlic
1 Medjool date, pitted
¾ teaspoon sea salt
¼–½ teaspoon chipotle chili powder

➤ Blend all ingredients in a blender until smooth.

SALAD

4 cups (136 g) packed chopped watercress
½ jicama, julienned
1 grapefruit, supremed
1 avocado, sliced
¼ cup (35 g) pumpkin seeds
¼ cup (4 g) chopped cilantro
Cayenne for garnish (optional)

➤ Toss watercress, jicama, grapefruit, and avocado in a bowl. Divide the mixture among four plates and drizzle with dressing. Top with pumpkin seeds and cilantro, and garnish with a dash of cayenne, if you like.

➤ If stored without dressing on it, this salad will keep for two to three days in the refrigerator.

HEALTH NOTE: Traditionally, watercress has been used to help digestion, fight bad breath and colds, and to clean the blood. It has a very high sulfur content and has been shown in laboratories to contain cancer–suppressing properties. It's also a good source of iodine, which makes it very beneficial to those suffering from hypothyroidism.

STRAWBERRY–SPINACH SALAD WITH SWEET BALSAMIC VINAIGRETTE

. . . .

I LIKE TO ADD EQUAL PARTS MESCLUN TO JAZZ IT UP, BUT FEEL FREE TO USE JUST SPINACH. THIS SALAD IS VERSATILE ENOUGH TO SERVE AT AN ELEGANT DINNER, A SUMMER PICNIC, A BRUNCH, OR AS A BREAKFAST SALAD.

. . . .

MAKES 4 SERVINGS

PREP TIME: 15 MINUTES

SALAD

4 cups (120 g) baby spinach
4 cups (120 g) mesclun mix
2 cups (290 g) sliced strawberries
¼ cup (120 g) red onion, thinly sliced with a mandoline or knife
¼ cup (36 g) chopped almonds

➤ Combine all salad ingredients in a large bowl and toss well.

DRESSING

¼ cup (59 ml) olive oil
2 tablespoons (28 ml) balsamic vinegar
1 teaspoon Dijon mustard
1 teaspoon agave
Salt and pepper to taste

➤ Whisk all the dressing ingredients together in a small bowl. Drizzle the dressing over individual salad servings as desired. Salad will keep one day.

COLORFUL CABBAGE SALAD

. . . .

I MADE A ZESTY VIETNAMESE–TYPE DRESSING TO GIVE THIS CRUNCHY, VIBRANT SALAD SOME MAJOR GINGER–GARLIC–LIME KICK. IT'S ONE OF MY GO–TO SALADS WHEN I'M ON A CLEANSE, AS IT HAS VERY LITTLE FAT (IF YOU OMIT THE PEANUTS) BUT IS VERY FILLING AND SATISFYING

. . . .

MAKES 4–6 SERVINGS

PREP TIME: 20 MINUTES

DRESSING

⅓ cup (78 ml) lime juice
2 tablespoons (30 ml) brown rice vinegar
1 tablespoon (15 ml) sesame oil
1 tablespoon (13 g) palm sugar or sweetener of choice
1 tablespoon (8 g) ginger, grated or ginger juice
1 teaspoon finely minced garlic
½ teaspoon sea salt
⅛ teaspoon cayenne

SALAD

5 cups (350 g/about 1 small head) packed, shredded red cabbage
1 cup (110 g) shredded carrots
½ cup (8 g) chopped cilantro
½ cup (13 g) chopped mint
⅓ cup (48 g) crushed raw wild jungle peanuts or roasted peanuts (not raw)

➤ Whisk all the dressing ingredients together in a small bowl.

➤ Combine salad ingredients in a large bowl.

➤ Pour in the dressing and toss well. Garnish with crushed peanuts. This salad will keep for three days in the refrigerator.

HEALTH NOTE: Cabbage is one of the most health–promoting vegetables out there. It's most revered for its anticancer, antitumor properties and is excellent at cellular detoxification and for the removal of carcinogens from our system.

CREAMY KALE SALAD WITH CAPERS AND HAZELNUTS

THE LOVELY GREEN AND PURPLE COLORS IN THIS SALAD MAKE IT A FAVORITE DISH TO SERVE FOR GUESTS. I ALSO LOVE HOW SIMPLE YET FLAVORFUL THIS SALAD IS. IT'S THE HAZELNUTS THAT REALLY MAKE IT FOR ME. IF YOU HAVE HAZELNUT OIL ON HAND, A LIGHT DRIZZLE WILL TAKE IT TO THE NEXT LEVEL.

MAKES 2–4 SERVINGS

PREP TIME: 25 MINUTES

2 large bunches flat or curly kale, stems removed and finely chopped
1 avocado, cubed
3 tablespoons (44 ml) lemon juice
1 teaspoon sea salt
1 cup (70 g) shredded purple cabbage
½ cup (88 g) chopped hazelnuts
2 tablespoons (17 g) capers

➤ Place the chopped kale in a bowl with avocado, lemon juice, and sea salt and massage it very well until the avocado becomes creamy and the kale becomes tender. Add cabbage, hazelnuts, and capers and toss well. Add additional seasonings or avocado if needed and serve. The salad will keep for one day.

HEALTH NOTE: I haven't met a raw foodist yet who doesn't include kale in their top three favorite ingredients list. Because of its dense nutrient profile, I like to stick kale in everything from juices to smoothies to salads. It's extremely high in bone–building vitamin K, antioxidants vitamin A and C, manganese and fiber, and is well regarded, along with other cruciferous vegetables, as an anticancer food. Its high sulfur content aids in the cellular detoxification process, which makes it the perfect cleansing food.

WINTERLAND SALAD

THIS IS A WONDERFUL MIX OF MY FAVORITE WINTER FRUITS TOSSED WITH AROMATIC FENNEL.

MAKES 4–6 SERVINGS

PREP TIME: 30 MINUTES

SALAD

2 fennel bulbs
2 green apples
1 cup (140 g) pomegranate seeds
½ cup (63 g) chopped walnuts
Fennel leaves for garnish

➤ Use a knife or mandoline to thinly slice the fennel bulb. Grate or julienne the apple. Next, toss all ingredients except the fennel leaves into a medium-size bowl.

DRESSING

½ cup (118 ml) orange juice
3 tablespoons (45 ml) apple cider vinegar
2 tablespoons (30 ml) olive oil
1½ tablespoons (16.5 g) prepared whole-seed mustard

➤ Whisk all the ingredients together in a small bowl and pour the dressing over the salad. Toss well and serve immediately. Garnish plated salads with fennel leaves.

➤ The salad will keep for two days in the refrigerator.

HEALTH NOTE: Fennel is a great source of vitamin C, potassium, folate, and fiber, and it's great for the digestive system.

SWEET CHILI DAIKON SALAD

THIS ULTRA SIMPLE SALAD MAKES A GREAT (AND VERY PRETTY) FIRST COURSE IF YOU'RE PUTTING TOGETHER AN ASIAN–INSPIRED MEAL. THE SWEET CHILI SAUCE IS NOT ONLY STUNNING TO LOOK AT OVER THE DAIKON NOODLES, BUT IT IS ALSO A FLAVORFUL COMPLIMENT TO THIS MILD RADISH.

MAKES 4 SERVINGS

PLAN AHEAD: MAKE HOT SAUCE (PAGE 142)

PREP TIME: 15 MINUTES

SWEET CHILI SAUCE

⅓ **cup (78 ml) Hot Sauce (page 142)**
¼ **cup (60 ml) brown rice vinegar**
2 **tablespoons (28 ml) agave or coconut nectar**
2 **tablespoons (30 ml) sesame or olive oil**
¼ **teaspoon sea salt**

➤ Whisk together or blend ingredients thoroughly.

SALAD

2 **large daikon radishes, peeled and spiralized or julienned**
1 **cup (16 g) chopped cilantro**
⅓ **cup (32 g) chopped almonds**

➤ Place prepared daikon on individual plates and garnish with cilantro and almonds. Dress with sweet chili sauce right before serving.

➤ Stored individually, Sweet Chili Sauce will last one week and the daikon will last three days in the refrigerator.

CHEF TIP: I used the Saladacco spiral slicer to make the daikon ribbons.

HEALTH NOTE: Daikon radish contains an abundance of digestive enzymes, making it a wonderful digestive aid, particularly in metabolizing fats. It's a very cleansing root vegetable that has been used traditionally as a diuretic and decongestant. Like others in its cruciferous family, it contains cancer–fighting properties and a good dose of vitamin C and potassium.

WATERMELON-TOMATO SALAD WITH FIG VINAIGRETTE

THIS SALAD IS AS TASTY AS IT IS LOVELY TO LOOK AT. I LOVE THE FRESH AROMA OF MINT AND BASIL WITH THE WATERMELON, AND THE FIG DRESSING TIES IT ALL TOGETHER WITHOUT BEING OVERWHELMING. IF YOU'RE ON A CLEANSE, YOU CAN SKIP THE DRESSING AND YOU'LL STILL HAVE A REALLY GREAT–TASTING DISH.

MAKES 4–6 SERVINGS

PLAN AHEAD: SOAK DRIED FIGS FOR 30 MINUTES

PREP TIME: 20 MINUTES

DRESSING

4 dried figs, soaked in ½ cup (120 ml) water for 30 minutes; reserve soak water
3 tablespoons (45 ml) balsamic vinegar
½ cup (118 ml) soak water
¼ cup (59 ml) olive oil
Salt and pepper to taste

➤ Blend all ingredients in a blender until smooth.

SALAD

8 cups (1,200 g) cubed watermelon
6 cups (1,080 g) cubed heirloom tomatoes of assorted colors
2 tablespoons (12 g) chopped mint
2 tablespoon (5 g) chopped basil
2–4 tablespoons (20–40 g) thinly sliced shallot

➤ Combine all ingredients in a large bowl, then scoop out into serving bowls. Drizzle the fig dressing over individual servings.

➤ This salad will keep for one day in the refrigerator.

SUNNY PEACH SALAD WITH CHIPOTLE-MAPLE DRESSING

SPICY–SWEET VINAIGRETTE OVER RIPE SUMMER PEACHES MAKES A GREAT COMBO IN THIS BEAUTIFUL
AND EFFORTLESS SALAD.

MAKES 4–6 SERVINGS

PREP TIME: 15 MINUTES

DRESSING

3 tablespoons (45 ml) olive oil
3 tablespoons (45 ml) balsamic vinegar
1½ tablespoons (25 ml) maple syrup
¼ teaspoon chipotle chili powder
¼ teaspoon sea salt

➤ Whisk together ingredients in a small bowl.

SALAD

6 cups (360 g) spring or mesclun mix
4 peaches, pitted and sliced
½ cup (56 g) chopped pecans
¼ cup (40 g) thinly sliced shallot

➤ Toss all ingredients in a large bowl and serve with
dressing on the side. This salad will keep for a day or two in
the refrigerator.

ROOT VEGETABLE SLAW

・・・

IF YOU REALLY WANT TO INDULGE, PICK UP A BOTTLE OF LEBLANC HAZELNUT OIL TO DRESS THIS COLORFUL, CRUNCHY SALAD. TO PREVENT BEETS FROM TURNING EVERYTHING PINK, I ADD THEM RIGHT BEFORE SERVING, BUT, IF YOU'RE THE ONLY WHO'S GOING TO SEE IT, FEEL FREE TO TOSS THEM IN WITH EVERYTHING ELSE.

・・・

MAKES 4 SERVINGS

PREP TIME: 40 MINUTES

SALAD

2 cups (300 g) julienned beets
2 cups (220 g) julienned carrots
2 cups (232 g) julienned daikon radish or celery root
2 green onions, thinly sliced, green parts only
¼ cup (40 g) dried cranberries or raisins
¼ cup (35 g) sunflower seeds

➤ Set the beets aside in their own small bowl and toss the remaining salad ingredients in a medium–size bowl.

DRESSING

¼ cup (59 ml) hazelnut or olive oil
¼ cup (59 ml) orange juice
2 tablespoons (30 ml) lemon juice
Salt to taste

➤ Whisk together all the dressing ingredients and pour the mixture over the salad, reserving a small amount for the beets.

➤ Add remaining dressing to the beets and gently incorporate them into the salad right before serving.

HEALTH NOTE: Root vegetables are a great source of minerals and antioxidants, as well as being excellent blood purifiers and liver detoxifiers. They also contain emotional and physical grounding energy that can make us feel more focused and powerful. It's a very similar energy to the kind meat eaters say they get from eating animal protein.

Mains

MUSHROOM TACOS

THESE TACOS ARE BURSTING WITH QUINTESSENTIAL MEXICAN FLAVORS LIKE JALAPEÑO, LIME, CILANTRO, AND AVOCADO. IF YOU'RE NOT A FAN OF MUSHROOMS, THE WALNUT MEAT FROM THE FIVE PEPPER CHILI (PAGE 123) IS A GREAT SUBSTITUTE.

MAKES 4 SERVINGS

PLAN AHEAD: YOU WILL NEED A BATCH OF QUICK PICKLED CABBAGE (SEE BELOW).

PREP TIME: 30 MINUTES

MARINATED MUSHROOMS

**4 cups (280 g) sliced shiitake or
    baby Portobello mushrooms**
2 tablespoons (28 g) tamari
1 small clove garlic, minced
1 tablespoon (15 ml) olive oil

➤ Place all of the ingredients into a large mason jar and shake vigorously or toss together in a bowl. Let the mushrooms sit while you make the remaining components.

AVOCADO SAUCE

⅓ cup (78 ml) water
1–2 tablespoons (15–30 ml) lime juice
½ teaspoon sea salt
½ avocado
1 clove garlic
**½ jalapeño pepper, with seeds,
    or cayenne pepper to taste**

➤ Blend all ingredients in a blender or food processor. Add more water or seasonings as needed. Transfer to a squeeze bottle or small bowl.

FILLING

1½ cups (225 g) Quick Pickled Cabbage
3–4 tomatoes, chopped
1 cup (16 g) chopped cilantro
⅔ cup (110 g) diced sweet onions
8 romaine leaves

➤ Fill each romaine leaf with marinated mushrooms. Top with the various fillings and drizzle with avocado sauce.

QUICK PICKLED CABBAGE

THIS IS A GREAT LITTLE CONDIMENT TO PUT ON THE MUSHROOM TACOS OR THROW INTO ANY WRAP OR SALAD FOR A LITTLE ZING AND SPLASH OF COLOR.

MAKES 8 SERVINGS

PREP TIME: 15 MINUTES

2 cups (140 g) shredded red cabbage
¼ cup (60 ml) apple cider vinegar
½ tablespoon (10 g) agave
pinch of sea salt

➤ Combine all ingredients into a bowl very well. Place a plate or bowl with weight (like a mason jar of water) on top of mixture and allow to sit for one to six hours. It will soften and release more liquid the longer you let it set.

➤ Will keep for 5 days in the refrigerator.

HEIRLOOM TOMATO STACKS

HERE'S A FUN AND EASY WAY TO ENJOY THE FRUITS OF SUMMER.

MAKES 4–6 SERVINGS

PLAN AHEAD: YOU WILL NEED ONE BATCH OF CILANTRO PESTO (PAGE 143) AND SUN–DRIED TOMATO SPREAD (PAGE 142).

PREP TIME: 10 MINUTES

1 batch Cilantro Pesto (page 143)
1 batch Sun Dried Tomato Spread (page 142)
4–6 large heirloom tomatoes of different colors
4 cups (120 g) spinach
1 cup (30 g) loosely packed basil leaves
Olive oil as needed
Fresh black pepper and sea salt to taste

➤ Slice tomatoes into ¼–inch thick rounds. Arrange 1 cup (30 g) of spinach on a serving plate. Spread the desired amount of Cilantro Pesto onto one tomato slice and place onto the bed of spinach, then place a couple of basil leaves on top. Spread desired amount of Sun–Dried Tomato Spread onto another slice of tomato and place it on top of the other tomato slice. Add additional basil or spinach leaves.

➤ Repeat these steps two more times, alternating spreads and different colors of tomato slices. When finished, drizzle the stacks with olive oil and add salt and pepper to taste and serve immediately.

THAI VEGGIE NOODLES

. . . .

NOODLES PLUS CREAMY CURRY SAUCE PLUS TONS OF VEGETABLES EQUALS ONE OF MY FAVORITE DISHES. YOU CAN PLAY AROUND WITH THE AMOUNT OF VEGGIES, BUT I LIKE TO GO CRAZY AND PILE THEM ON. IF YOU CAN'T FIND KELP NOODLES IN THE REFRIGERATOR SECTION OF YOUR LOCAL HEALTH FOOD STORE, YOU CAN REPLACE THEM WITH TWO ADDITIONAL ZUCCHINI.

. . . .

MAKES 4–6 SERVINGS

PREP TIME: 45 MINUTES

1 12-ounce (340 g) package kelp noodles

SAUCE

½ cup (112 g) almond butter
¼ cup (59 ml) water
¼ cup (59 ml) tamari
2 tablespoons (30 ml) brown rice vinegar
2 tablespoons (15 g) red Thai curry paste
½ teaspoon crushed red pepper (optional)
2 tablespoons (28 ml) agave nectar or
 few drops liquid stevia
1 tablespoon (8 g) grated ginger or ginger juice
1 clove garlic

VEGETABLES

1 lemon
4 zucchinis, peeled
1 red bell pepper, diced
2 large carrots, julienned
2 green onions, green parts sliced thinly
2 cups (100 g) bean sprouts
½ cup (20 g) Thai or traditional basil, shredded
4 cups (120 g) spinach

➤ Rinse and loosen the kelp noodles and place them in a bowl. Cover the noodles with water and squeeze the juice from the lemon into it. Allow them to soak for 30 minutes.

➤ While the noodles are soaking, make your sauce by processing all the sauce ingredients until smooth in a blender.

➤ After 30 minutes, rinse the noodles and place them into a medium–size bowl. It's helpful to cut noodles with kitchen scissors, as they tend to be crazy long.

➤ Spiralize the zucchini with a vegetable spiralizer or use a peeler to turn them into ribbons. Combine the zucchini with the kelp noodles and toss with sauce. Serve the zucchini–noodle mixture on a bed of spinach and top with vegetables and shredded basil. This will last two days in the refrigerator.

CHEF TIP: Warm this dish by placing noodles in a dehydrator for one hour at 145˚ F (62.8˚ C) or warm in a saucepan on low heat, stirring frequently. For a lightly cooked version, place noodles and vegetables in a large saucepan or pot and warm gently for 5–10 minutes, stirring constantly.

BUTTERNUT SQUASH NOODLES WITH SAGE CREAM

THIS A VERY DELICATELY FLAVORED DISH COMPARED TO MANY OF THE BOLD, SPICY RECIPES IN THIS BOOK. I LOVE THE SUBTLETY OF THE SAGE CREAM AND MILDLY NUTTY FLAVOR OF THE NOODLES. THE SEASONED PISTACHIOS ADD A NICE TEXTURAL CRUNCH WITH A SMALL PUNCH OF SMOKY, GARLICKY FLAVORS.

MAKES 4 SERVINGS

PLAN AHEAD: SOAK 1 CUP (150 G) CASHEWS FOR 2 HOURS

PREP TIME: 30 MINUTES

NOODLES

2 whole butternut squash
2 cups (60 g) micro greens

➤ Peel and spiralize the squash using a vegetables spiralizer or shred them into ribbons using a vegetable peeler. Toss micro greens in with the noodles.

CHEF TIP: I prefer to make a fine angel hair–type noodle with butternut squash, instead of a thick spaghetti-size noodle for this recipe.

SAGE CREAM

1 cup (150 g) cashews, soaked 2 hours
¼ cup (55 g) hemp seeds
¾ cup (176 ml) water
2 tablespoons (32 g) chickpea miso paste
2–3 tablespoons (30–44 ml) lemon juice
1 tablespoon (12 g) nutritional yeast
1 clove garlic
¼–½ teaspoon sea salt
½ teaspoon agave
4 fresh sage leaves

➤ Process all the ingredients in a blender until smooth. Adjust seasonings if needed.

SEASONED PISTACHIOS

½ cup (50 g) coarsely chopped pistachios
½ teaspoon olive oil
¼ teaspoon smoked paprika
¼ teaspoon garlic powder
⅛–¼ teaspoon sea salt

➤ Put all ingredients in a small bowl and mix thoroughly using your fingers.
➤ To assemble, place noodles in a bowl or on individual plates. Top with the desired amount of sage cream and sprinkle with pistachios. Edible pansies are optional, but a nice touch.

Zucchini Noodles, Two Ways

YOU CAN USE EITHER GREEN ZUCCHINI OR YELLOW SUMMER SQUASH TO MAKE AWESOME NOODLES. IT'S UP TO YOU IF YOU WANT THEM WITH OR WITHOUT THE PEEL. I PREFER WITHOUT IF I'M SERVING RAW–CURIOUS GUESTS. IF YOU HAVE A VEGETABLE SPIRALIZER, YOU CAN MAKE SPAGHETTI–LIKE NOODLES IN A JIFFY. I LIKE TO MAKE THEM ON THE THICKER SIDE, AS OPPOSED TO ANGEL HAIR, AS THEY CAN BECOME WATERY QUITE QUICKLY ONCE YOU PUT THE SAUCES ON THEM. IF YOU DON'T OWN A SPIRALIZER, USE A VEGETABLE PEELER TO TURN THEM INTO WIDE FETTUCCINE–STYLE NOODLES.

HERE ARE TWO CLASSIC SAUCES THAT WORK BEAUTIFULLY. EACH SAUCE WILL BE ENOUGH FOR FOUR MEDIUM ZUCCHINIS. DON'T DRESS NOODLES UNTIL READY TO SERVE, AS THEY WILL SOFTEN AND WEEP. SERVE WITH PARMESAN CHEESE.

PASTA MARINARA

MAKES 4 SERVINGS

PREP TIME: 15 MINUTES

½ red bell pepper, seeded and chopped
2 tablespoons (14 g) sun dried tomato powder
1–2 tablespoon (15–30 ml) olive oil
2 tablespoons (5 g) fresh basil, or 1 teaspoon dried
1 tablespoon (8 g) fresh oregano, or
   1 teaspoon dried
½ Medjool date
2 cloves garlic
½–¾ teaspoon sea salt or to taste
¼ teaspoon crushed red pepper
3 cups (540 g) chopped tomatoes

➤ Blend all of the ingredients except tomatoes in a food processor until smooth. Add tomatoes and pulse until incorporated but still a little chunky.

➤ Spiralize or peel zucchinis into ribbons and toss with marina sauce. Garnish with pine nuts, olives, or diced bell peppers.

CHEF TIP: Make sun–dried tomato powder by grinding sun–dried tomatoes in a spice grinder.

PESTO PASTA

MAKES 4 SERVINGS

PREP TIME: 10 MINUTES

2 cups (80 g) basil leaves, packed
¼ cup (59 ml) olive oil
3–4 cloves garlic, crushed
½–1 teaspoon sea salt
½ cup (110 g) hemp seeds or raw pine nuts

➤ Place all ingredients except hemp seeds (or pine nuts) in a food processor and blend until smooth. Add hemp seeds and pulse a few times until incorporated.

➤ Spiralize or peel zucchinis into ribbons and toss with pesto. Garnish with diced tomatoes, pine nuts, olives, or diced bell peppers.

PARMESAN CHEESE

½ cup (75 g) cashews
1 clove garlic
1 teaspoon nutritional yeast
¼ teaspoon sea salt

➤ Use a spice grinder to combine all ingredients.

FIVE-PEPPER VEGETABLE CHILI

DON'T BE INTIMATED BY THE NAME: THIS ISN'T OVERLY SPICY, BUT IT DOES HAVE A LITTLE BIT OF A KICK. I LOVE THE UNDERTONES OF CACAO, CINNAMON, AND SMOKED PEPPERS, BUT YOU CAN SIMPLIFY THIS RECIPE BY OMITTING THEM. THIS IS A GREAT DISH THE WHOLE FAMILY WILL LOVE, AND IT CAN EASILY BE WARMED OVER THE STOVETOP IF YOU HAVE GUESTS WHO PREFER THEIR CHILI COOKED. THIS IS EXTRA NICE TOPPED WITH A DOLLOP OF CRÈME FRAICHE (PAGE 140) OR CUBED AVOCADO.

MAKES 6 SERVINGS

PREP TIME: 45 MINUTES

SAUCE

1 cup (235 ml) water
½ red bell pepper, seeded and chopped
3 tablespoons (42 g) sun-dried tomato powder (see chef's tip, page 126)
2 tablespoons (30 ml) orange juice
2 Medjool dates, pitted
1 tablespoon (7.5 g) Mexican chili powder
1 tablespoon (15 g) olive oil
½ tablespoon (4 g) cacao powder
1 teaspoon tamarind paste
1 teaspoon sea salt
1 small clove garlic
½ teaspoon onion powder
¼ teaspoon cinnamon
¼ teaspoon ancho chili powder
⅛ teaspoon chipotle chili powder

➤ Blend all ingredients in a blender until smooth. Adjust seasonings as desired.

WALNUT MEAT

1½ cups (180 g) walnuts
2 teaspoons chili powder
1 teaspoon cumin
2 tablespoons (28 g) tamari

➤ Put all ingredients in a food processor and process until well combined. I like to keep it a little chunky for texture.

VEGGIES

1 cup (30 g) (120 g) diced zucchini
1 cup (30 g) (180 g) diced tomatoes
1 cup (175 g) corn kernels
1 cup (110 g) shredded carrots
¼ cup (40 g) diced white or yellow onions
1 jalapeño, seeded and diced

➤ Put all ingredients in a large bowl and mix. Add sauce and walnuts and combine well.

CHEF TIP: The sauce and walnut meat can be made the day before to cut down on prep time. When serving, you can warm this in the dehydrator for one hour at 145° F (63° C) or on the stovetop at low heat stirring frequently.

CHIPOTLE NOT–CHICKEN SALAD WRAPS

••

THIS WRAP HAS A HEARTY FILLING THAT CAN BE EATEN ON ITS OWN, ADDED TO A SALAD, OR SPREAD OVER A FLAX CRACKER. FOR A NICE VARIATION, IT CONVERTS WELL INTO A CURRY SALAD—OR KEEP IT SIMPLE AND REPLACE THE SPICE WITH CAPERS.

••

MAKES 4 SERVINGS

PLAN AHEAD: SOAK SUNFLOWER SEEDS FOR 4–6 HOURS.

PREP TIME: 20 MINUTES

1 cup (30 g) (145 g) sunflower seeds, soaked and drained
¼ cup (59 ml) water
2 tablespoons (15 ml) apple cider vinegar
¾ teaspoon sea salt
½ teaspoon chipotle chile powder
½ teaspoon paprika
¾ cup (75 g) chopped celery
¾ cup (113 g) sweet cherry tomatoes, sliced
¼ cup (40 g) chopped red onion
1 avocado, cubed
4 large collard leaves

➤ In a food processor, blend sunflower seeds and water until you have a pâté. Scrape down the sides of the container as needed until you achieve desired consistency. Add vinegar, sea salt, chipotle powder, and paprika, and process again. Transfer the mixture to a bowl and stir in celery, tomatoes, and red onions. Gently fold in avocados.

➤ Lay one collard leaf on a cutting board. Use a knife to cut off the protruding bottom stem. Fillet the thickest part of the remaining stem very carefully. This will make the leaf more pliable.

➤ Spoon the mixture onto the bottom third of the collard leaf. Roll the leaf up from the bottom and tuck in the sides as you go along to make a nice, tight wrap.

➤ You can store the salad mixture in an airtight container for two or three days in the refrigerator.

COOKED VARIATION: Rather than roll the collard leaves, serve them on toasted sprouted bread with vegan cheese.

HEALTH NOTE: Sunflower seeds are an excellent source of vitamin E as well as magnesium and selenium. They're also very affordable and versatile and a great alternative to nuts. I toss them into salads and use them in place of nuts for many of my savory dishes.

LEMONY GARLIC BROCCOLI BOWL

THIS IS A HEARTY DISH THAT CAN BE ENJOYED WARM OR COLD. I LIKE IT WITH A LITTLE SIDE OF HOT SAUCE (PAGE 142).

MAKES 4–6 SERVINGS

PLAN AHEAD: SOAK ½ CUP (73 G) ALMONDS OVERNIGHT IN WATER AND RINSE WELL (OPTIONAL).

PREP TIME: 20 MINUTES

TAHINI DRESSING

⅔ **cup (167 g) raw tahini paste**
⅔ **cups (167 ml) water**
½ **cup (118 ml) lemon juice**
3 **cloves garlic**
1 **teaspoon sea salt**
¼ **teaspoon black pepper**
⅛ **teaspoon cayenne**

➤ Blend all ingredients in a blender or food processor until smooth.

BROCCOLI BOWL

5 **cups (355 g) broccoli florets,**
   cut into small bite–size pieces
2 **cups (176 g) bean sprouts**
1 **cup (110 g) shredded carrots**
½ **cup (73 g) chopped almonds**

➤ Cover broccoli in hot water for several seconds then plunge it into cold water. This will soften it and make it more palatable. Next, mix vegetables and almonds in a large bowl and serve with tahini dressing.

➤ Stored separately, Tahini Dressing will keep for one week and Broccoli Bowl mixture will keep for two or three days in the refrigerator.

CHEF TIP: You can give the sauce an ethnic kick by adding in a little Thai or curry paste when blending or replace the sauce with Nacho Cheese (page 86) or your favorite raw sauce.

COOKED OPTION: Steam vegetables gently or serve them with cooked quinoa.

GINGER MISO HAND ROLLS

THIS VERSATILE RECIPE IS AN EASY WAY TO THROW SOMETHING TOGETHER WITHOUT RESORTING TO THE TYPICAL SALAD. YOU COULD FILL THESE HAND ROLLS WITH ANY OF YOUR FAVORITE GREENS AND VEGETABLES AND EVEN USE DIFFERENT DRESSINGS, THOUGH THE GINGER MISO DRESSING GIVES IT THE ASIAN TOUCH. KEEP THE SAUCE ON HAND SO YOU CAN MAKE A QUICK MEAL IN MINUTES ANYTIME.

MAKES 4 SERVINGS

PLAN AHEAD: MAKE ALMOND OR CASHEW MILK (PAGE 59) (OPTIONAL)

PREP TIME: 20 MINUTES

GINGER MISO DRESSING

⅓ cup (80 ml) olive oil
3–4 tablespoons (45–60 ml) Almond or
   Cashew Milk (page 59) or water
2½ tablespoons (43 g) chickpea miso
2 tablespoons (28 ml) agave or coconut nectar
1½ tablespoons (12 g) grated ginger
1 tablespoon (7.5 ml) balsamic vinegar

➤ Blend all ingredients in a blender until smooth.

NORI WRAPS

4 untoasted nori sheets
8 green lettuce leaves
2–3 carrots, julienned or shredded
1 beet, julienned or shredded
2 small avocados, sliced
2 cups (100 g) sprouts of choice

➤ To make the hand roll, hold the nori sheet with the shiny side down on your palm in a diamond position. Lay two pieces of lettuce in the upper corner of the diamond.

➤ Add remaining filling as desired.

➤ Drizzle with ginger miso sauce.

➤ Fold the right corner of the nori sheet over the filling, and fold bottom corner upward over filling.

➤ Fold the left corner over the filling to close. You can use a tiny bit of water to seal the nori sheet closed.

➤ Serve immediately. Ginger Miso dressing will keep for one week in the refrigerator.

HEALTH NOTE: Nori sheets are the most popular type of seaweed. They are rich in vitamins, minerals, and amino acids and have been regarded in Japanese culture as a beauty food. The majority of store brands are toasted, but you may be able to find raw nori sheets at some health food stores as well as online. If you can't find it raw, toasted is still a great option.

1

OLD THE NORI SHEET WITH THE SHINY SIDE DOWN ON
OUR PALM IN A DIAMOND POSITION. LAY TWO PIECES OF
TTUCE IN THE UPPER CORNER OF THE DIAMOND.

2

ADD REMAINING FILLING AS DESIRED.

3

DRIZZLE WITH GINGER MISO SAUCE.

4

OLD THE RIGHT CORNER OF THE NORI SHEET OVER
HE FILLING, AND FOLD BOTTOM CORNER UPWARD OVER
LLING.

5

FOLD THE LEFT CORNER OVER THE FILLING TO CLOSE. YOU
CAN USE A TINY BIT OF WATER TO SEAL THE NORI SHEET
CLOSED.

6

SERVE IMMEDIATELY.

VIETNAMESE SALAD ROLLS

ONE OF THE THINGS I LOVE ABOUT VIETNAMESE CUISINE IS THE USE OF FRESH HERBS. I'M HEAVY HANDED WITH THE MINT AND CILANTRO IN THESE ROLLS WHEN I MAKE THEM FOR MYSELF. TRY EXPERIMENTING WITH OTHER VEGETABLES AND ELEMENTS SUCH AS CUCUMBERS, BELL PEPPER, BASIL, RADISH, OR FRESH YOUNG THAI COCONUT MEAT FOR A HEARTIER ROLL.

MAKES 4 SERVINGS

PREP TIME: 30 MINUTES

SWEET AND SOUR MANGO SAUCE

MAKES 1 CUP (30 G) (305 G)

1 cup (175 g) chopped mango
3 tablespoons (45 ml) agave or sweetener of choice
3 tablespoons (44 ml) lime juice
½ tablespoon (4 g) grated ginger
1 clove garlic
½ teaspoon crushed red pepper flakes (optional)
¼ teaspoon sea salt

➤ Blend ingredients in a blender or food processor. Adjust seasonings as desired.

SPICY TAHINI SAUCE

MAKES 1 CUP (30 G) (305 G)

½ cup (120 g) tahini
⅓ cup (78 g) water
3 tablespoons (54 g) tamari
2 tablespoons (30 ml) lemon juice
2 tablespoons (28 ml) agave nectar or
   few drops liquid stevia
1 tablespoon (15 g) red Thai curry paste (optional)
1 tablespoon (8 g) grated ginger or ginger juice
1 clove garlic
½ teaspoon crushed red pepper

➤ Blend all ingredients in a blender or food processor until smooth

SALAD ROLLS

4 large chard, cabbage, or collard leaves
1 head romaine or other green lettuce
2 cups (220 g) shredded carrots
2 cups (100 g) bean sprouts
4 green onions, sliced longwise, green parts only
⅔ cup (17 g) mint leaves
⅔ cup (17 g) chopped cilantro

➤ Lay a chard, cabbage, or collard leaf on a plate or cutting board. Fillet the thick stem carefully using a paring knife. This will allow you to roll the leaf easier without it breaking.

➤ Lay two leaves of lettuce on the inside of the chard leaf and fill with remaining ingredients as desired. Lay another couple of lettuce leaves over the filling and roll. Serve with sauces.

COOKED VARIATION: You can wrap your rolls in rice paper. Also known as bingh mah, rice paper can be found at any Asian market and some health food stores. Rice paper is very easy to use. Simply dip a sheet into hot water for a few seconds then remove, shake off excess water, and lay it on a flat surface. Add your fillings and roll carefully. For a heartier cooked meal, add in organic tempeh.

MEAT AND CHEESE PIEROGIES

• •

COMING FROM AN EASTERN EUROPEAN BACKGROUND, I GREW UP ON PIEROGIES AND WANTED TO CREATE SOMETHING REMINISCENT OF WHAT MY MOM USED TO MAKE. THESE MAKE GREAT FINGER FOOD FOR PARTIES OR CAN BE SERVED WITH A SALAD FOR DINNER. THE CHEESE IS OUT OF THIS WORLD AND CAN BE USED WITH WRAPPERS OTHER THAN TURNIP. TRY THINLY SLICED BEETROOT, ZUCCHINI, OR JICAMA FOR ALTERNATIVE WRAPPERS.

• •

MAKES 6 SERVINGS

PREP TIME: 20 MINUTES

PLAN AHEAD: SOAK CASHEWS AND PINE NUTS FOR 2 HOURS AND MAKE CRÉME FRAICHE (PAGE 140)

MEAT FILLING

1 cup (30 g) (120 g) walnuts or pecans
1 tablespoon (15 g) tamari
1 teaspoon lemon juice
½ teaspoon cumin
¼ teaspoon onion powder
¼ teaspoon garlic powder
⅛ teaspoon black pepper

➤ Mix all of the ingredients in a food processor until the mixture looks like minced meat. Scrape down the sides of the container as needed.

CHEESE FILLING

½ cup (75 g) cashews, soaked 2 hours
½ cup (68 g) pine nuts, soaked 2 hours
1–2 tablespoons (15–30 ml) lemon juice
1½ tablespoons (18 g) nutritional yeast
¼ teaspoon salt

➤ Mix all ingredients in a food processor until well combined. Scrape down sides of the container as needed.

WRAPPER

1 large round turnip, peeled

➤ To make the wrapper, use a mandoline or knife to slice the turnip into very thin rounds.

TOPPING

Crème Fraiche (page 140)
Chopped chives
Microgreens for garnish

➤ To assemble, place a small dollop of meat and cheese filling on the rounds and then pinch to close like a pita pocket. Top with Crème Fraiche and chives and serve over a bed of microgreens.

➤ These pierogies will last three days in the refrigerator.

Fermented Foods and Beverages

Civilizations have been using fermentation as a way to preserve food for ages. It wasn't until this past century, though, that people discovered how health promoting it really was. The bacteria created by fermentation is imperative for building a strong immune system, manufacturing B vitamins and the neurotransmitter serotonin, and very helpful in reducing inflammation and clearing up skin issues and allergies. We need beneficial bacteria to break down the food we eat so it can be absorbed into the body. If you don't have good digestion, you're not going to get all the vitamins and minerals you need and will eventually suffer from a nutritional deficiency even if you're eating all the right foods. Probiotics are used extensively in autism treatment, as research has shown that children with autism always have major digestive issues. Many people report that they have fewer sugar cravings, as it helps get sugar-feasting candida under control.

Most people are deficient in beneficial bacteria because of our modern lifestyle. Some major causes are:

- Antibiotic use
- Poor diet
- Chlorinated water
- Excess stress

We can remedy this deficiency easily with lifestyle changes and adding living fermented foods to our diet every day. They are much more effective than a manufactured probiotic pill or sugar-laden processed yogurt. I've included a few easy recipes you can make, such as kraut and kefir. I suggest having a little with each meal, as soon as you wake up, and before bed.

NOTE: Before preparing any of the recipes make sure you sterilize all of the jars and utensils that you will be using. You can do this by letting them sit in boiling water for a few minutes or running them through the dishwasher.

WATER KEFIR

Water kefir grains are a symbiotic culture of bacteria and yeast (SCOBY). Sounds yummy, right? Well, actually, it is. Kefir grains are an easy and inexpensive way to make your own fermented probiotic beverage that tastes delicious and is really good for you. The end product is similar to soda and has a host of great health properties. If you like kombucha, you'll love making your own water kefir. I find the taste much more pleasing and it takes only two to three days to make as opposed to kombucha's two to three weeks.

Kefir grains are a white, translucent color, but depending on the type of sugar you feed it, it can change to different shades of brown. You can order your grains online or find someone locally who is giving them away. Kefir grains multiply like rabbits, so once you start making your own kefir you're going to be looking for people to share the surplus with. You may also eat your extra grains by adding them to smoothies.

YOU'LL NEED THE FOLLOWING MATERIALS:

¼ cup (48 g) water kefir grains
Quart or liter jar with lid
Cheesecloth or coffee filter
Rubber band
Sugar (any organic crystallized sugar, coconut palm sugar, brown sugar, evaporated cane juice, maple syrup, or agave—but do not use honey. The antibacterial properties will eventually kill the grains.)

SOME TIPS FOR MAKING GREAT KEFIR:

➤ Kefir grains like mineral–rich water. Spring or well water is ideal, but if you don't have access, you can use reverse osmosis or other filtered water. The lack of minerals in reverse osmosis and filtered water will eventually starve your grains. Adding an occasional teaspoon of black-strap molasses will keep your grains thriving.

➤ Avoid tap water. The chlorine will ruin the grains.

➤ Kefir grains are more active when they have oxygen, so cover the jar opening with cheesecloth, a coffee filter, or a loose lid when you are in the first fermentation stage. After you strain out your grains, cap the jar tightly to allow the gas bubbles to build up and create a great fizzy drink.

➤ Sometimes it takes a couple weeks to get brand–new grains firing. Adding a few pieces of dried fruit and a quarter of a lemon is a good way to make them more active. You can put grains in a food processor or blender to break them into smaller pieces so you have a more active surface area.

➤ Grains are heat sensitive. Don't use hot water or leave them near an intense heat source.

➤ Use only unsulfured dried fruit, preferably without added oils.

➤ There is an art to making water kefir. The grains can change from batch to batch and season to season. The ideal ratio of sugar to water is 1 tablespoon (13 g) to 1 cup (235 ml) of water. Sometimes your grains will react well to a type of sugar you're using and then they stop. Sometimes they love ginger, then they don't. They get bored, so mix it up and keep things interesting. Sometimes I use half of one type of sugar and half of another and change up the dried fruit each batch.

(continued)

The light kefir on the right is in the first fermentation stage. This is the Ginger Ale Kefir made using organic white crystallized sugar, hence its light appearance. The kefir on the left is in the second fermentation stage. The grains have been strained and the jar has a tight fitting lid. I made this Fruity Kefir using goji berries and coconut palm sugar, which gave it a dark brown color. Bubbles should be very visible at this stage.

If you want to put them into storage, you can keep your grains in a glass quart jar with water and 2 tablespoons (30 ml) of maple syrup in the refrigerator. Change the water every two weeks so you don't accidentally pickle your grains.

➤ You may want to avoid kefir or any fermented drinks that contain a SCOBY, like kombucha, if you are on an anticandida cleanse. Some kefir grains can contain bacterial strains that feed candida and may sabotage your efforts if you are currently dealing with overgrowth. Once you have it under control, you should have no problem enjoying kefir.

BASIC WATER KEFIR

**3 tablespoons (13 g) crystallized sugar,
maple syrup, agave, or coconut palm sugar**
Filtered water
¼ cup (48 g) water kefir grains

➤ In your quart jar, add sugar and a small amount of hot water. Stir until the sugar dissolves.

➤ Fill the jar three–quarters of the way (about 3 cups, or 705 ml) with room–temperature water and add the kefir grains. Using a rubber band, secure a piece of cheesecloth or a coffee filter over the opening and store the jar in a warm place (72–78° F or 22–26° C) in your house away from sunlight.

➤ Allow the grains to ferment for twenty–four to forty–eight hours. Check the flavor at twenty–four hours. If it's too sweet give it another twelve hours or so. Ideally it should be tart but not too sour. This is called the first fermentation.

➤ When ready, strain the grains and pour the kefir back into the jar. Place a tight–fitting lid over the jar and allow the kefir to sit another twelve hours or so to become fizzy. This is called the second fermentation.

WARNING: Don't forget about your kefir! I've had jars explode after forty–eight hours because of the pressure buildup.

➤ Store your kefir in the refrigerator and enjoy. It can last several weeks and will continue to slowly ferment.

VANILLA SODA KEFIR

1 cup (235 ml) Basic Water Kefir
1 teaspoon vanilla extract
Stevia to taste

➤ Mix the ingredients in a glass and enjoy.

FRUITY KEFIR

**3 tablespoons (13 g) crystallized sugar, agave,
maple syrup, or palm sugar**
Filtered water
¼ cup (48 g) water kefir grains
**2 tablespoons (15 g) of unsulfured dried fruit (cherries,
goji berries, mulberries, apricot, cranberries,
pineapple, mango, or fig)**

➤ Follow the same instructions for Basic Water Kefir but add dried fruit to the first fermentation. You can leave the fruit in for the entire time if you choose. I remove them after about four to five days.

GINGER ALE KEFIR

Filtered water
¼ cup (48 g) water kefir grains
**3 tablespoons (13 g) crystallized sugar, agave,
maple syrup, or palm sugar**
3 slices of fresh ginger

➤ Follow the same instructions for Basic Water Kefir. Add ginger to the first fermentation and leave it in as long as you want.

CHERRY SODA KEFIR

1 cup (235 ml) Basic Water Kefir
1 teaspoon cherry extract
Stevia to taste

➤ Mix the ingredients in a glass and enjoy.

COCONUT KEFIR

START YOUR DAY OFF WITH ¼ CUP (59 ML) OF KEFIR TO IMPROVE DIGESTION AND BOOST YOUR IMMUNE SYSTEM. YOU CAN ALSO ADD IT TO SMOOTHIES.

MAKES 8 SERVINGS

3 ½ cups (823 ml) fresh young Thai coconut water (about 4 coconuts)
Kefir starter (I recommend Body Ecology) or ⅓ cup (78 ml) store–bought coconut kefir

➤ If using kefir starter, warm coconut water in a saucepan to about 90–98° F (32–37° C). Dissolve one packet (5 g) of kefir starter in the coconut water.

➤ If using store-bought coco kefir, you can skip to the next step and add it into the jar without heating.

➤ Pour the coconut water into a 1-quart (946 ml) glass jar and close tightly. Allow the kefir to ferment for thirty-six to forty-eight hours at room temperature 72–75° F (22–24° C).

➤ Fermented coconut water will become milky white and will form bubbles at the top. The kefir should be fizzy, and the taste should be slightly tart and tangy.

➤ You can start another batch of kefir by adding ⅓ cup (78 ml) of fermented coconut kefir to fresh coconut water and repeating the fermentation process. It is best to make the transfer within three days.

➤ This can be done about seven times before you need to use a new kefir culture starter.

➤ Store coconut kefir in the refrigerator and consume within one week.

CULTURED BEET–APPLE SALAD

THIS RECIPE WAS ADAPTED FROM GINA LAVERDE'S (BLISSEDLIFE.COM) "BEET IT" RECIPE. HER BLOG IS A WEALTH OF INFORMATION ABOUT RECOVERING FROM AUTISM WITH FERMENTED FOODS. I EAT AT LEAST ½ CUP A DAY OF THIS SALAD WITH A DOLLOP OF CRÈME FRAICHE (PAGE 140) FOR WHAT I LIKE TO CALL "SWEDISH BREAKFAST." EAT IT AS A SNACK, SIDE DISH, OR THROW ON TOP OF A GREEN SALAD.

MAKES 16 SERVINGS

PREP TIME: 45 MINUTES

EQUIPMENT

½ gallon (1.9 L) mason jar with lid

1 packet Body Ecology cultured vegetable starter
¼ cup (59 ml) warm water
1 ½ cups (350 ml) filtered water
2 lbs (.9 kg) about 3 red beets, shredded
3 large green apples, shredded
1 small bunch dill, chopped
¼ cup (59 ml) lemon juice
1 tablespoon (5 g) caraway seeds (optional)
1 tablespoon (18 g) sea salt
2–3 beet greens or cabbage leaves

➤ Dissolve culture starter in 1/4 cup (59 ml) water warmed to 90° F (32° C) water. Combine with additional 1 1/2 cups (350 ml) water.

➤ Mix beets, apples, dill, lemon juice, caraway seeds and sea salt in a large bowl. Toss well. Tightly pack vegetables into the mason jar using your hands (you might want to wear gloves) or use a vegetable masher. Pour water over vegetables and pack firmly again. Top off mixture with clean beet greens or cabbage leaves.

➤ Close jar with lid and let ferment at room temperature, away from sunlight, for five to fourteen days. The longer it sits the more tart it will get. Give it a daily taste test to see how you like it. Store in the refrigerator with a lid. It will continue to slowly ferment and bubble. As long as mixture is covered in the brine, it will last several weeks in the refrigerator.

JALAPEÑO KRAUT

YOU MAY HAVE GATHERED FROM READING THIS BOOK THAT I LIKE IT HOT. THIS SAUERKRAUT HAS SOME NICE HEAT TO IT, BUT IF YOU PREFER IT TO BE MILDER, REMOVE THE SEEDS FROM THE PEPPERS BEFORE MIXING THEM IN.

MAKES 16 SERVINGS

PREP TIME: 45 MINUTES

EQUIPMENT

½ gallon (1.9 L) mason jar with lid

1 packet Body Ecology cultured vegetable starter
1 cup (235 ml) water
1 large head green cabbage, shredded
1 small bulb white or yellow onion, diced
1 cup (110 g) shredded carrots
1 cup (30 g) (116 g) sliced daikon radish
4 red jalapeño or Fresno peppers, chopped with seeds
2 tablespoons (36 g) sea salt
1 packet culture starter
1–2 cabbage leaves

➤ Dissolve culture starter in ¼ cup (59 ml) water warmed to 90° F (32° C). Combine with additional 1 cup (235 ml) water.

➤ Mix cabbage, onion, carrots, daikon, peppers, and sea salt in a large bowl and massage with your hands for a few minutes. Best to use gloves so you don't get pepper burns. Pack mixture tightly into jar.

➤ Pour water into jar so you have 1 inch (25 cm) of brine above your mixture. Add more water if needed. Lay cabbage leaves on top of mixture and press down firmly.

➤ Close jar with a lid and allow to sit at room temperature (70–76°F [21–24°C]), away from sunlight, for five to fourteen days. The longer it sits the more sour it will get. When ready, store in the refrigerator with a lid. It will continue to slowly ferment and bubble. As long as mixture is covered in the brine it will last several weeks in the refrigerator.

Condiments

ORANGE–CRANBERRY–APPLE RELISH

THIS MAKES A GREAT HOLIDAY SIDE THAT'S PERFECTLY SWEET AND TART. DOUBLE THE RECIPE IF YOU'RE GOING TO A BIG SHINDIG BECAUSE EVERYONE WILL BE WANTING SECONDS.

MAKES 6 SERVINGS

PREP TIME: 15 MINUTES

1½ cups (159 g) fresh or frozen cranberries, thawed
2 red delicious apples, chopped (peel if waxed)
½ cup (120 g) coarsely chopped walnuts
2 tablespoons (30 ml) orange juice
2 tablespoons (30 ml) agave
½ teaspoon orange zest
Dash ground cloves (optional)

➤ Place cranberries into a food processor and pulse several times until berries break down into small pieces. Be careful not to overprocess. Transfer the cranberry bits to a mixing bowl.

➤ Place the apples into the food processor and pulse again several times until broken down but still chunky. Again, take care not to overdo it. Transfer the apples to the mixing bowl with the cranberries and stir in walnuts, orange juice, agave, orange zest, and cloves. Mix well before serving.

➤ Relish will last three days in the refrigerator.

HEALTH NOTE: Studies have shown that it is not the juice but the whole cranberry that has so many healing properties, such as helping to inhibit bacteria that cause urinary tract infections and ulcers, reducing inflation and bad cholesterol, and providing relief for asthma sufferers.

CRÈME FRAICHE

CRÈME FRAICHE IS JUST A FANCY WAY OF SAYING SOUR CREAM, BUT THIS IS WAY BETTER. YOU CAN USE IT IN MANY OF THE SOUPS, FIVE PEPPER CHILI (PAGE 123), MUSHROOM TACOS (PAGE 112), AND CULTURED BEET APPLE SALAD (PAGE 139).

MAKES 12 SERVINGS

PLAN AHEAD: SOAK 1 CUP (150 G) CASHEWS FOR 2 HOURS

PREP TIME: 5 MINUTES

1 cup (150 g) cashews, soaked for 2 hours
½ cup (118 ml) water
¼ cup (59 ml) lemon juice

➤ Blend all ingredients in a blender until very smooth. Chill to firm.

➤ This will keep in the refrigerator for one week.

SWEET ALMOND RICOTTA

HONEY AND ALMONDS MAKE ME SWOON. I GET LOCAL ORANGE BLOSSOM HONEY, WHICH HAS A LOVELY FLORAL FLAVOR, FROM THE FARMER'S MARKET. STRICT VEGANS WILL WANT TO SUBSTITUTE THE HONEY WITH AGAVE, WHICH STILL TASTES WONDERFUL. USE THIS RICOTTA WITH THE STONE FRUIT SALAD (PAGE 40) OR AS A DESSERT TOPPING.

MAKES 8 SERVINGS

PLAN AHEAD: BLANCH ALMONDS BY SOAKING THEM IN BOILING WATER FOR 5 MINUTES, THEN DRAINING THEM AND COVERING THEM WITH COLD WATER. WHEN COOLED, PINCH OFF AND DISCARD THE SKINS. SOAK ALMONDS FOR 8–12 HOURS BEFORE USING.

PREP TIME: 10 MINUTES

¾ cup (71 g) almonds, blanched and soaked
¼ cup (20 g) young Thai coconut meat
2½ tablespoons (50 g) honey or agave nectar
½ teaspoon almond extract
½ vanilla bean, scraped
Dash sea salt
¼ cup (59 ml) water

CHEF TIP: You'll get the best results using a high–power blender with a plunger, such as the Vitamix. If you don't own a powerful blender, you will have better results using a food processor.

➤ Process all ingredients in a blender or food processor. You will have to stop and start several times to scrape the sides and push the mixture back into the blades. Add 1 tablespoon (15 ml) at a time of additional water, if needed, to keep blades moving. Don't use too much or you will lose the fluffy ricotta consistency.

➤ This will keep for one week in the refrigerator.

HEALTH NOTE: Almonds contain almost 8 grams of protein per ¼ cup (59 ml), more than the typical egg. They also contain heart-healthy monounsaturated fat, vitamin E, magnesium, calcium, and potassium. For centuries, mothers in India have been giving their children a few soaked almonds every morning to help improve cognitive function. Recent studies have confirmed that almonds are great brain food and support the nervous system.

HEMP SEED BUTTER

I GAVE UP PEANUT BUTTER WHEN I WENT RAW DUE TO THE CARCINOGENIC AFLATOXINS, SO I WAS OVERJOYED TO FIND A BUTTER I LOVE JUST AS MUCH. IT'S NUTTY, SUBTLY SWEET, SALTY, AND PERFECTLY CREAMY. THIS IS SOME SERIOUSLY GOOD STUFF THAT IS RIDICULOUSLY NUTRITIOUS. SPREAD IT OVER BANANAS, APPLE SLICES, CELERY STICKS, CRACKERS, OR SPROUTED BREAD. OR JUST EAT IT STRAIGHT OUT OF THE JAR LIKE I DO.

MAKES 12 SERVINGS

PREP TIME: 5 MINUTES

2 cups (336 g) hemp seeds
¼ teaspoon sea salt
1½ tablespoons (22.5 ml) olive or flaxseed oil
2–3 tablespoons (30–45 ml) yacon syrup or agave or coconut nectar

➤ Place hemp seeds in a food processor with sea salt. While seeds are processing, drizzle oil followed by the yacon syrup into the container and process until fully homogenized with a buttery consistency. Scrape down the sides of the container if needed.

➤ Store in an airtight jar in the refrigerator for up to two weeks.

HOT SAUCE

I LOVE SRIRACHA AND OTHER HOT SAUCES, BUT UNFORTUNATELY MANY ARE MADE WITH PRESERVATIVES. THIS HOT SAUCE IS FRESH, TASTY, AND ADDITIVE FREE. MUCH OF THE HEAT OF PEPPERS COMES FROM THE SEEDS, SO IF YOU WANT A MILDER HOT SAUCE, JUST REMOVE MOST OF THE SEEDS. IF YOU LIKE IT FLAMING HOT, THEM LEAVE THEM IN.

MAKES ABOUT ½ CUP (110 G)

PREP TIME: 10 MINUTES

1 red bell pepper
1 Fresno or red jalapeño or Serrano pepper, chopped, with seeds
1 teaspoon apple cider vinegar
1 teaspoon coconut palm sugar
1 clove garlic
¼–½ teaspoon sea salt

➤ Blend until smooth. Adjust seasonings to taste. This will keep for one week in an airtight container in the refrigerator.

MANGO SALSA

THIS MAKES A GREAT LITTLE SIDE TO MUSHROOM TACOS (PAGE 112) OR USE IT AS A DIP OR ON TOP OF SALADS.

MAKES 4 SERVINGS

PREP TIME: 15 MINUTES

1 cup (175 g) finely diced mango
½ diced avocado
½ finely diced red jalapeño, seeded
1 tablespoon (10 g) finely diced red onion
½ tablespoon chopped cilantro (.5 g)
1–2 tablespoons (15–30 ml) lime juice
Salt to taste (optional)

➤ Mix all the ingredients in a small bowl. This will keep for two days in the refrigerator.

SUN–DRIED TOMATO SPREAD

THIS IS A LIGHTER SPREAD THAN A NUT PATE OR PESTO AND HAS A BRILLIANT TOMATO–CITRUS FLAVOR. I USE THIS IN MY TOMATO STACKS (PAGE 115), BUT IT'S GREAT ON CRACKERS AND CRUDITÉS.

MAKES 6 SERVINGS

PLAN AHEAD: SOAK CASHEWS AND SUN–DRIED TOMATOES.

PREP TIME: 15 MINUTES

½ cup (75 g) cashews, soaked 2 hours
2 cloves garlic, minced
⅔ cup (37 g) sun–dried tomatoes, soaked two hours in 1 cup (235 ml) water, reserved
¼ cup (59 ml) soak water
2–4 tablespoons (30–59 ml) orange juice
½ teaspoon sea salt

➤ Place cashews and garlic in a food processor and process until coarse. Add tomatoes and process until puréed, scraping down the sides of the container as needed with a spatula.

➤ Add ¼ cup (59 ml) of soaking water, orange juice, and sea salt and process again until smooth. Adjust seasonings as needed.

➤ This will keep for one week in the refrigerator.

Clockwise: Cilantro Pesto, Sun–Dried Tomato Spread, and Herbed Pecan Pâté.

HERBED PECAN PÂTÉ

THIS RICH, DIVINE SPREAD IS GREAT ON CRACKERS AND CELERY STICKS. I'VE EVEN ROLLED THEM INTO "MEATBALLS" AND TOSSED THEM INTO MY RAW ITALIAN SPAGHETTI DISHES.

MAKES 12 SERVINGS

PREP TIME: 15 MINUTES

2 cups (220 g) pecans
2 tablespoons (30 ml) lemon juice
2 tablespoons (28 g) tamari
1 tablespoon (3 g) chopped chives
½ tablespoon (1.2 g) fresh chopped thyme
½ tablespoon (2 g) fresh chopped oregano
1 clove garlic, minced

➤ Place pecans in a food processor and grind into a flour. Add remaining ingredients and process until well combined. Scrape the sides of the container with a spatula as needed.

➤ The pâté will last one week in an airtight container in the refrigerator.

CILANTRO PESTO

THIS FLAVORFUL PESTO IS SO DIFFERENT FROM YOUR USUAL BASIL VARIETY. CILANTRO AND PUMPKIN HAVE VERY STRONG FLAVORS THAT WORK INCREDIBLY WELL TOGETHER. I USE THIS IN MY TOMATO STACKS (PAGE 115) BUT IT ALSO MAKES A GREAT SPREAD FOR CRACKERS, FLATBREAD, OR CUCUMBER ROUNDS.

MAKES 6 SERVINGS

PREP TIME: 10 MINUTES

1 cup (16 g) firmly packed fresh cilantro
1 small clove garlic, crushed
½ cup (140 g) pumpkin seeds
¼ cup (59 ml) olive oil
½ jalapeno or ¼ serrano pepper, seeded and chopped
1 teaspoon lime or lemon juice
¼ teaspoon sea salt

➤ Place all ingredients in a food processor and process until smooth. Use a spatula to scrape down sides of container as needed. This will last four days in an airtight container in the refrigerator.

HEALTH NOTE: Cilantro contains chemical compounds that bind to heavy metals from the organs and tissue and escorts them out of the body. This natural chelator is a great herb for those with mercury fillings or who cook with aluminum. Cilantro is also a liver cleanser, is great for digestion, reduces bad cholesterol, and has some antibacterial properties that may even reduce the risk of salmonella exposure.

Desserts

SUPERFOOD SEED BAR

• •

THIS NUT–FREE, MINERAL–RICH BAR IS JUST HEAVENLY. IT CONTAINS ALL MY FAVORITE SUPERFOODS HELD TOGETHER WITH CREAMY TAHINI AND COCONUT OIL. BE CAREFUL YOU DON'T OVERDO IT: IT IS HARD TO STOP WITH JUST ONE. HIGH IN PROTEIN, ZINC, CALCIUM, AND ESSENTIAL FATTY ACIDS, THIS MAKES A GREAT POST–WORKOUT OR ANYTIME SNACK, AND I LOVE THAT IT'S NOT TOO SWEET. I USE LOW–GLYCEMIC COCONUT NECTAR, BUT YOU CAN USE YACON SYRUP, MAPLE SYRUP, OR AGAVE IF YOU CAN'T FIND IT IN YOUR AREA.

• •

MAKES 16 SERVINGS

PREP TIME: 20 MINUTES

½ cup (118 ml) coconut nectar
⅓ cup (80 g) raw tahini
¼ cup (59 ml) coconut oil, warmed to liquid
1 vanilla bean, scraped or pinch of vanilla powder
1 cup (140 g) pumpkin seeds
1 cup (30 g) (145 g) sunflower seeds
½ cup (75 g) goji berries
½ cup (80 g) shredded coconut
¼ cup (36 g) black sesame seeds
¼ cup (24 g) cacao nibs
¼ cup (24 g) hemp seeds
Pinch of salt

➤ In a blender, process coconut nectar, tahini, coconut oil, and vanilla until smooth and set aside.

➤ In a medium-size mixing bowl, combine remaining dry ingredients. Add in coconut nectar mixture and mix well using your hands. I recommend wearing gloves. It'll be pretty sticky.

➤ Take half of the mixture and place it in a food processor. Process until the mixture breaks down into very small pieces. Transfer it back to the mixing bowl and combine it with the remaining mixture using your hands.

➤ Press the mixture into an 8 x 8 inch (20 x 20 cm) pan lined with parchment paper or plastic wrap and place in the freezer until firm, about thirty to sixty minutes.

➤ Cut bars into desired pieces and store in the refrigerator or freezer if you like them chewier. This will keep for one to two months in the refrigerator or freezer.

ORANGE-ALMOND TRUFFLES

THIS IS THE PERFECT LAST–MINUTE DESSERT YOU CAN WHIP UP IF YOU HAVE UNEXPECTED COMPANY COMING OVER OR NEED TO BRING A LITTLE SOMETHING TO A PARTY. THE DUSTING OF CACAO REALLY TIES THE ORANGE AND ALMOND FLAVORS TOGETHER BEAUTIFULLY.

MAKES 20 TRUFFLES

PREP TIME: 20 MINUTES

2 cups (145 g) almonds
1 cup (178 g) Medjool dates, pitted
2 tablespoons (30 ml) orange juice
2 teaspoons orange zest
¼ teaspoon sea salt
⅛ teaspoon vanilla powder, or ½ teaspoon vanilla extract
1–2 tablespoons (15–28 g) cacao powder

➤ Place all ingredients except cacao powder into a food processor and process until well combined and the mixture begins to stick together. You can check for stickiness by pressing the mixture between your fingers.

➤ Scoop out one heaping tablespoon at a time and roll into twenty balls using your hands.

➤ Sprinkle cacao powder onto a flat clean surface, such as a dinner plate, and roll the truffles in it until coated. Shake off the excess cacao.

➤ Truffles can be served immediately or chilled to firm up. Store in an airtight container in the refrigerator for two weeks or in the freezer for two months.

CHOCOLATE HAYSTACKS

THESE AWESOMELY DELICIOUS TREATS ARE SUPER–SIMPLE TO MAKE AND WILL BRIGHTEN ANYONE'S DAY. I USE LONGER COCONUT THREADS TO GIVE IT THAT HAYSTACK LOOK, BUT YOU CAN USE THE FINELY SHREDDED COCONUT WITH THE SAME GREAT RESULTS. JAZZ IT UP WITH SOME CHOPPED NUTS OR HEMP SEEDS FOR A LITTLE NUTRITION BOOST.

MAKES 12 SERVINGS

PREP TIME: 15 MINUTES

⅔ cup (66 g) cacao powder
½ cup (118 ml) maple syrup
¼ cup (59 ml) coconut oil, warmed to liquid
½ vanilla bean, scraped, or small pinch of vanilla powder
¼ teaspoon sea salt (optional)
2 cups (160 g) shredded coconut

➤ Blend cacao powder, maple syrup, coconut oil, vanilla, and salt in a blender or food processor until smooth.

➤ In a bowl, hand mix the shredded coconut with chocolate mixture.

➤ Line a plate with parchment paper. Use a spoon or melon scoop to form twelve to fourteen individual haystacks on the parchment paper. Freeze for thirty minutes or until firm.

➤ The haystacks can be stored in the refrigerator or freezer for one month.

CARROT–APPLE CUPCAKES

THIS IS SO MUCH BETTER THAN ANY STORE–BOUGHT CARROT CAKE I'VE EVER HAD. I USE DRIED APPLES TO HELP ABSORB THE MOISTURE FROM THE CARROTS AND ABSOLUTELY LOVE THE WAY THE TARTNESS BRIGHTENS THE FLAVOR. THE DREAMY CREAM CHEESE FROSTING IS THE MAIN STAR, THOUGH. GO AHEAD AND SLATHER IT ON; YOU'LL HAVE PLENTY FOR THE CUPCAKES AND SOME LEFT OVER TO EAT WITH A SPOON.

MAKES 12–16 SERVINGS

PREP TIME: 45 MINUTES PLUS 4 HOURS TO CHILL

CREAM CHEESE FROSTING

½ cup (75 g) cashews, soaked 2 hours
¼ cup (59 ml) coconut oil, warmed to liquid
¼ cup (59 ml) water
¼ cup (59 ml) xylitol or agave
2 tablespoons (30 ml) lemon juice
½ tablespoon (7.5 ml) vanilla extract
2 teaspoons lecithin powder

➤ Combine all ingredients except lecithin powder in a blender until very smooth. Add lecithin and blend again.

➤ Chill for four hours or until completely firm

CARROT–APPLE BASE

⅔ cup (80 g) walnuts
1¼ cup (106 g) dried apples
⅔ cup (73 g) carrot pulp or shredded carrots, squeezed to get rid of excess liquid
⅔ cup (119 g) packed Medjool dates, pitted
1 teaspoon cinnamon
½ teaspoon ground ginger
1 small vanilla bean, scraped, or ½ tablespoon (7.5 ml) vanilla extract
¼ teaspoon sea salt
Dash nutmeg
Dash clove
½ cup (120 g) chopped walnuts
⅓ cup (48 g) raisins
Additional chopped walnuts for garnish

➤ Grind walnuts into a coarse meal in a food processor. Add apples, carrots, and dates and process until incorporated. Add cinnamon, ginger, vanilla, nutmeg, and clove, sea salt and process until you have a dough.

➤ Transfer the dough to a bowl and mix in chopped walnuts and raisins. Then press the dough into twelve mini cupcake cups lined with cupcake wrappers. They will have some height to them, so shape them into little mounds. You could also make them flatter and smaller by putting them into sixteen cupcakes cups instead of twelve.

➤ If you don't own a mini cupcake pan, you can press the mixture into a loaf pan lined with parchment paper to make a mini cake.

➤ Frost the mini cupcakes or loaf by hand or use a pastry bag and top with chopped walnuts. Leftover frosting can be stored in the freezer.

CHERRY BOMB CUPCAKES

CAROB POWDER RESEMBLES CACAO POWDER BUT IT'S SWEET, NOT BITTER LIKE CACAO, AND CONTAINS LESS FAT. IT'S A GREAT OPTION FOR PEOPLE AVOIDING THE STIMULATING EFFECTS OF CACAO. TRY NOT TO EAT ALL THE FROSTING BEFORE YOU ICE YOUR CUPCAKES. IT'S PRETTY ADDICTIVE!.

MAKES 12–16 SERVINGS

PREP TIME: 40 MINUTES

FROSTING

2 large avocados
⅔ cup (69 g) untoasted, raw carob powder
½ cup (118 ml) xylitol
2 teaspoons vanilla extract
Dash salt

➤ Place all ingredients in a food processor and mix very well, scraping down the sides with a spatula as needed. It should become a thick cream. If it doesn't thicken, add a little more carob and xylitol.

➤ Transfer the mixture to a bowl and chill in the refrigerator while you make the cupcake base.

BASE

2 cups (240 g) walnuts
⅓ cup (34 g) untoasted, raw carob powder
¼ cup (45 g) pitted dates
1 teaspoon cherry extract
Dash salt
¼ cup (61 g) dried cherries, chopped
1 tablespoon (15 ml) water

➤ Put walnuts into a food processor and grind into a flour. Then add dates, carob powder, cherry extract, and a dash of salt and process until the mixture starts to stick together. Transfer to a mixing bowl and add cherries and water. Use your hands to combine mixture.

➤ Pack the mixture firmly into twelve mini cupcake tins lined with cupcake wrappers. Decorate your cupcakes with frosting using a pastry bag or by hand using a small spatula. If you ice by hand, you will have excess frosting.

➤ Alternatively, you can bypass the cupcake tins and press the mixture into a loaf pan lined with parchment paper and hand frost. The cupcakes will keep for one week in the refrigerator.

GERMAN CHOCOLATE CUPCAKES

I MADE THIS RECIPE FOR MY HUSBAND, WHO REQUESTS GERMAN CHOCOLATE CAKE EVERY YEAR FOR HIS BIRTHDAY. HE SAID I "KNOCKED IT OUT OF THE BALLPARK" WITH THESE CUPCAKES, AND I AGREE. THEY'RE PRETTY AMAZING.

MAKES 12–16 SERVINGS

PREP TIME: 30 MINUTES

FROSTING

½ cup (113 g) pecan or almond butter
½ cup (40 g) shredded dried coconut
¼ cup (59 ml) agave
1 tablespoon (15 ml) water
1 teaspoon vanilla extract
Pinch sea salt
⅓ cup (37 g) finely chopped pecans
Shaved chocolate for garnish (shave a raw or organic store–bought chocolate bar with a vegetable peeler to make curly chocolate sprinkles)

➤ In a small bowl, mix by hand all the ingredients except chopped pecans and shaved chocolate. Add a tablespoon of water if needed.

➤ Place the mixture in the freezer or refrigerator to chill while you make the cupcake base.

BASE

2½ cups (300 g) walnuts
¾ cup (134 g) packed Medjool dates
½ cup (50 g) cacao powder
Pinch sea salt

➤ Place the walnuts in a food processor and grind into a flour. Add dates, cacao, and sea salt and process until the mixture starts to stick together. Don't overprocess or it will become too oily. If the mixture isn't sticking together well, transfer it to a bowl, add 1 tablespoon (15 ml) of water, and mix well with your hands.

➤ When the mixture is the right consistency, press it into a twelve–tin mini cupcake pan lined with cupcake wrappers. They will have some height to them. Shape the tops into little mounds. If you choose, you can make them flatter and create about sixteen smaller cupcake cups instead.

➤ If you don't own a mini cupcake pan you can press the mixture into a loaf pan lined with parchment paper to make a mini cake.

➤ Stick the cupcake pan or loaf pan in the freezer or refrigerator for twenty to thirty minutes to firm up.

ASSEMBLY

➤ Generously frost cupcakes using a butter knife or small offset spatula. Top with chopped pecans and shaved chocolate.

➤ Store cupcakes in the refrigerator for two weeks or in the freezer for one month.

SUGAR-FREE CHOCOLATE PUDDING/ICE CREAM

THIS IS A DREAMY AND VERSATILE TREAT YOU CAN ENJOY TWO WAYS, EITHER AS A LUSCIOUS PUDDING OR AS A FROZEN TREAT. MY CLIENTS HAVE STATED THAT AS AN ICE CREAM, IT'S "LIFE CHANGING!" I ESPECIALLY LOVE IT STRAIGHT FROM THE ICE CREAM MAKER WHEN IT HAS THAT SOFT SERVE TEXTURE. HAVING A HIGH-SPEED BLENDER IS VERY HELPFUL TO GET A SILKY-SMOOTH CONSISTENCY. THE KEY IS TO BLEND IT FOR AT LEAST TWO TO THREE MINUTES. SERVE IT WITH CHOPPED STRAWBERRIES—OR JUST ABOUT ANY TOPPING.

MAKES 8–10 SERVINGS

PLAN AHEAD: MAKE UNSWEETENED ALMOND OR CASHEW MILK (PAGE 59)

PREP TIME: 20 MINUTES

2 cups (80 g) young Thai coconut meat (about 3 coconuts)
1 cup (235 ml) unsweetened Almond or Cashew Milk (page 59)
½–⅔ cup (118–157 ml) xylitol
½ cup (50 g) cacao powder
¼ cup (59 ml) coconut oil, warmed to liquid
½ tablespoon (7.5 ml) vanilla extract
Dash sea salt

➤ Blend all ingredients in a blender for at least two to three minutes until smooth. You may need to stop and start a few times. Add more almond milk if needed to keep things going, but you want to keep it thick.

➤ Add more cacao or sweetener if you want a more intense flavor.

➤ Chill the mixture in the refrigerator before serving. It will keep for four days in the refrigerator.

TO MAKE ICE CREAM

➤ Because treats don't taste as sweet when they're frozen, add an additional 2 tablespoons (28 g) of xylitol when blending. Chill in the refrigerator and then process in an ice cream maker according to manufacturer's instructions.

➤ This ice cream will keep for several weeks in the freezer—but I doubt it'll last that long!

BANANA—BERRY SOFT SERVE

NO FAT, NO SUGAR ADDED. JUST NAKED FROZEN FRUIT MAKES THIS A GREAT TREAT FOR KIDS AS WELL AS FOR THOSE ON A CLEANSE. I'VE LISTED THREE WAYS TO MAKE THIS ULTRA SIMPLE DESSERT.

MAKES 2 SERVINGS

PLAN AHEAD: FREEZE 1 CUP (150 G) EACH OF BANANA CHUNKS AND MIXED BERRIES (BLUEBERRIES, STRAWBERRIES, RASPBERRIES).

PREP TIME: 10 MINUTES

1 cup (150 g) frozen banana chunks
1 cup (150 g) frozen mixed berries

VITAMIX METHOD

➤ Blend the frozen fruit on high for several seconds while using the plunger to push the fruit into the blades. It will be loud and wild, but you'll get a perfectly whipped dessert.

FOOD PROCESSOR METHOD

➤ Place the fruit in a food processor and process until softened. Scrape down the sides of the container as needed. It won't be completely homogenized, but I actually prefer it that way.

MASTICATING JUICER METHOD

➤ If you have a masticating gear juicer like a Champion, Omega 8005, or Greenstar, you can run the frozen fruit through the chute using the blank screen to create a perfect soft serve.

Ice Pops

Ice pops are ridiculously easy to make and so much fun to eat. You can buy molds from the store, use an ice cube tray, or use any sort of small, unique containers you might have laying around, such as small yogurt cups or cupcake tins. When I developed these recipes I used the Norpo brand Popsicle maker, which makes ten three–ounce pops. I love that it's BPA free, has a classic shape, and only cost a few bucks.

I made four different ice pop recipes, but I'm sure you could come up with a hundred new ones. Any kind of fruit purée will work. Just add a little extra sweetener, as they won't taste as sweet once they're frozen.

➤ TIPS ON MAKING PERFECT POPS:
- Only use food–grade wooden sticks. You can also find reusable BPA–free plastic sticks or bamboo sticks.
- Avoid glass molds. They are difficult to remove and could shatter.
- Chill your pops for two hours so they become slushy before inserting the stick; otherwise it will be crooked.
- Remove pops by holding molds under a hot running water for several seconds to loosen.
- You can transfer your pops to a freezer bag or container when ready or just store in the molds.

FUDGE POPS

MAKES 9–10 SERVINGS

PLAN AHEAD: SOAK YOUR CASHEWS FOR TWO HOURS IF YOU DON'T HAVE A HIGH–POWER BLENDER.

PREP TIME: 10 MINUTES

1½ cups (353 ml) Almond or Cashew Milk (page 59) or water
1 cup (150 g) cashews, soaked 2 hours
⅓ cup (78 ml) plus 1 tablespoon (15 g) xylitol, or ⅓ cup (80 ml) agave
¼ cup (25 g) cacao powder

➤ Put all ingredients into a blender and process until very smooth. Pour the liquid into pop molds and allow it to chill for one to two hours or until slushy. Insert wood holders and chill until firm.

➤ To remove the pops, hold the molds under hot running water for a few seconds or allow to sit at room temperature for a few minutes if you can wait that long.

STRAWBERRY FIELDS ICE POPS

• •

THESE ARE ICIER THAN MY OTHER POPS, BUT THEY ARE CHOCKFUL OF STRAWBERRY CHUNKS. THEY'RE ALWAYS THE FIRST ONES TO DISAPPEAR AT A PARTY.

• •

MAKES 9–10 POPS

PLAN AHEAD: MAKE ALMOND OR CASHEW MILK (PAGE 59)

2 cups (340 g) chopped strawberries, divided
1½ cups (352.5 ml) Almond or Cashew Milk (page 59)
¼ cup (59 ml) or more xylitol or sweetener of choice
1 teaspoon vanilla extract

➤ Blend 1 cup (30 g) (170 g) strawberries with nut milk and sweetener until smooth. Mash the remaining strawberries with a fork. Distribute equally among pop molds followed by the puree.

➤ Allow the pops to chill for one to two hours or until slushy, then insert wood holders and chill until firm.

➤ To remove the pops, hold the molds under hot running water for a few seconds or allow to sit at room temperature for a few minutes.

ORANGE DREAM POPS

MY FAVORITE POP EVER. SWEET AND TART CITRUS WITH A HINT OF CREAMY COCONUT...I COULD EAT THE ENTIRE BATCH BY MYSELF OVER A HOT SUMMER WEEKEND.

MAKES ABOUT 10 POPS

1 cup (80 g) young Thai coconut meat
2 ½ cups (600 g) orange juice
2 teaspoons orange zest
2 tablespoons (28 ml) vanilla extract
A touch of lemon juice, or sweeten to taste

➤ Put all ingredients into a blender and process until very smooth. If your mixture is foamy from blending, allow it to sit for five to ten minutes and then use a large spoon to skim off the foam.

➤ Pour the liquid into pop molds and allow it to chill for one to two hours or until slushy. Insert wooden sticks and chill until firm.

➤ To remove pops, hold the molds under hot running water for a few seconds or allow them to sit at room temperature for a few minutes.

SWEET BASIL ICE POPS

THIS IS AN ICE POP FOR A SOPHISTICATED PALATE. IT'S MORE LIKE AN ICE CREAM WITH A DELICATE FLAVOR OF BASIL. THESE POPS ARE A DELICIOUS CHOICE WHEN YOU HAVE A YEN FOR SOMETHING UNIQUE.

MAKES 10 POPS

PLAN AHEAD: SOAK THE CASHEWS FOR 2 HOURS IF YOU DON'T HAVE A HIGH-POWER BLENDER AND MAKE ALMOND MILK (PAGE 59) IF YOU WOULD LIKE THEM A LITTLE CREAMIER.

PREP TIME: 10 MINUTES

1 cup (150 g) cashews, soaked
2 cups (470 ml) Almond Milk (page 29) or water
1 cup (30 g) loosely packed basil
⅓ cup (78 ml) plus 1 tablespoon (15 g) xylitol,
   or ⅓ cup (78 ml) agave

➤ Place all ingredients into a blender and process until very smooth. If your mixture is foamy from blending, allow it to sit for five to ten minutes, then use a large spoon to skim off the foam.

➤ Pour the liquid into pop molds and allow it to chill for one to two hours or until slushy. Insert wooden sticks and chill until firm.

➤ To remove pops, hold the molds under hot running water for a few seconds or allow to sit at room temperature for a few minutes.

OATMEAL WALNUT RAISIN COOKIES

MAKE SURE THERE ARE NO CHILDREN IN THE ROOM WHEN YOU TASTE THESE CHUNKY, CHEWY COOKIES BECAUSE YOU MIGHT START CUSSING AT HOW INCREDIBLY TASTY THEY ARE. OR AM I THE ONLY ONE WHO SWEARS LIKE A SAILOR WHEN I EAT SOMETHING CRAZY GOOD?

MAKES 20 COOKIES

PREP TIME: 20 MINUTES

2 cups (200 g) walnuts
1 cup (30 g) (178 g) packed Medjool dates, pitted (soak for 15 minutes if they are very dry)
1 cup (80 g) rolled oats
½ tablespoon (7.5 ml) vanilla extract
1 teaspoon cinnamon
¼ teaspoon sea salt
½ cup (73 g) raisins

ADDITIONAL
⅔ cup (80 g) chopped walnuts
¼ cup (20 g) rolled oats

➤ Put the walnuts into a food processor and process until they almost turn into walnut butter. Add the dates and process again until it becomes doughlike, then add oats, vanilla, cinnamon, and sea salt and process until well incorporated and doughy.

➤ Transfer the mixture to a bowl and stir in the raisins.

➤ Take one heaping tablespoon of mixture at time in your hands and shape into twenty balls. If your mixture isn't sticking together, sprinkle it with two teaspoons of water.

➤ Spread chopped walnuts and oats onto a clean surface work area. Press the balls into the chopped walnuts and oats and shape into cookies.

➤ Chill the cookies in the freezer for a chewier texture or in the refrigerator for a softer cookie.

➤ Store in an airtight container in refrigerator or freezer for one month.

EASY APPLE PIE WITH SALTED CARAMEL SAUCE

SOMETIMES YOU NEED AN APPLE PIE IN YOUR MOUTH *RIGHT NOW*. THIS COULDN'T BE SIMPLER AND YET IS, SO INCREDIBLY DELICIOUS. THE SALTED CARAMEL MIGHT BE ONE OF THE BEST RECIPES TO COME OUT OF MY KITCHEN, AND THE BEST PART IS IT'S LOW GLYCEMIC.

MAKES 4 SERVINGS

PREP TIME: 20 MINUTES

CRUST

1 cup (30 g) (120 g) walnuts
3 tablespoons agave (45 ml) or coconut nectar
¼ teaspoon cinnamon
Dash sea salt

➤ Process walnuts in a food processor until they become a flour. Add the remaining ingredients and blend until smooth.

APPLE FILLING

2 cups (300 g) shredded or spiralized apples, with excess liquid gently squeezed out
2–3 tablespoons agave (45 ml) or coconut nectar
2 tablespoons (30 ml) lemon juice
⅛ teaspoon cinnamon

➤ Combine all the ingredients in a bowl. Adjust flavors as desired.

SALTED CARAMEL

⅓ cup (78 ml) coconut nectar
3 tablespoons coconut oil (44 ml), warmed to liquid
½ tablespoon (7.5 g) almond butter
Pinch salt

➤ Use a whisk or blend ingredients in a mini blender until smooth.

TO ASSEMBLE

➤ Use a knife or spoon to spread the crust mixture onto four serving plates. Form the crusts into 3–inch (7.5 cm) disks. Top the crusts with a ½ cup (123 g) each of apple filling and drizzle with caramel sauce. Use a squeeze bottle to make fun designs on the plate. Serve immediately.

➤ The crust and caramel will last for two weeks in the refrigerator.

CHEF TIP: I used the Saladaccio to spiralize the apples in the photograph.

WILD BLUEBERRY–MEYER LEMON CHEESECAKE SQUARES

I GOT TIRED OF REGULAR ROUND CHEESECAKES, SO I CREATED THIS CHUNKY VERSION USING A CRUST AND TOPPING VERY SIMILAR TO THE OATMEAL RAISIN WALNUT COOKIES (PAGE 158). DON'T FRET IF YOU CAN'T FIND WILD BLUEBERRIES OR MEYER LEMONS—I JUST WANTED TO GIVE THIS A FANCY NAME. MEYER LEMONS ARE SLIGHTLY SWEETER THAN REGULAR LEMONS, BUT EITHER KIND WORKS JUST AS WELL HERE. AS FOR BLUEBERRIES, I ACTUALLY PREFER USING THE FROZEN ONES BECAUSE OF THE JUICE THAT RESULTS FROM THAWING THEM OUT. WILD BLUEBERRIES ARE SMALLER IN SIZE BUT TASTE VERY MUCH LIKE CULTIVATED BLUEBERRIES SO USE WHATEVER YOU CAN FIND OR AFFORD AT YOUR LOCAL MARKET.

MAKES 16 SERVINGS

PLAN AHEAD: SOAK ½ CUP (75 G) CASHEWS IN WATER FOR 2 HOURS.

Prep time: 40 MINUTES, AND 1 TO 2 HOURS TO CHILL

CRUST

2 cups (240 g) walnuts or pecans
¼ cup (36 g) raisins
⅛ teaspoon sea salt

➤ Combine all the crust ingredients in a food processor for twenty to twenty–five seconds. Press the mixture between your fingers to see if it sticks together. If not, process the crust a few seconds longer. Be careful not to process for too long—otherwise it will release too much oil.

➤ Press the crust firmly and evenly into an 8x8 pan lined with parchment paper or plastic wrap.

TOPPING

1 cup (30 g) (120 g) walnuts or pecans
⅓ cup (50 g) raisins
⅓ cup (59 g) Medjool dates
⅛ teaspoon sea salt
½ cup (40 g) rolled oats (optional)

➤ In same food processor that you just used to make the crust, add nuts, raisins, dates, and sea salt and process until the mixture begins to clump and stick together. Process longer than you did the crust, but be careful not to overdo it.

➤ Transfer the mixture to a bowl and stir in the oats. Set the topping aside while you make the cheesecake layer.

CHEESECAKE

1 cup (236 ml) coconut oil, warmed to liquid
½ cup (75 g) cashews, soaked 2 hours
⅓ cup (38 ml) lemon juice
½ cup (118 ml) xylitol or agave
¼ cup (59 ml) water
½ tablespoon (3 g) lemon zest
1 teaspoon vanilla extract
1 tablespoon (7.5 g) lecithin powder
 (use 2 tablespoons (40 g) if using agave)
2 cups (310 g) fresh or frozen wild blueberries, thawed

➤ Blend all of the ingredients except the lecithin and blueberries until very smooth. Add the lecithin and blend again. Pour the mixture over the crust.

➤ Top the cheesecake mixture evenly with blueberries, pressing them gently into the cheesecake. Evenly spread the topping mixture over the berries.

➤ Chill the cheesecake in the refrigerator or freezer for an hour or two or until firm. It will keep for three to four days in the refrigerator or one month in the freezer.

CHEF TIP: You can use other berries or fruits in place of blueberries, such as cherries, peaches, or mango. You can also tone down the lemon flavor to your liking.

Raw & Simple Snack Ideas

Here are a few quick and easy snack ideas. Note: Many health food stores carry dehydrated kale chips, raw flax, chia, and nori crackers, and you can find a plethora of different varieties online. They're great to have around when you want something salty and crunchy. I especially love to crumble them over my salads.

- Sliced apple rings with almond butter and Cherry-Hemp Muesli (page 44), pictured on the opposite page

- Banana smothered in 2 tablespoons (28 g) Hemp Seed Butter (page 141) or almond butter and a sprinkling of cacao nibs

- Large flax cracker topped with mashed avocado, sliced tomatoes, and a dash of sea salt, pepper, and spirulina. Top with sprouts (optional)

- Mushroom caps (stems removed) filled with Smoky Guacamole (page 86)

- Romaine leaf filled with Smokey Guacamole (page 86) or sliced avocado and tomato and topped with a dash of spirulina and crumbled flax crackers or kale chips

- 1 large heirloom tomato, cubed and topped with chopped basil, sea salt, and pepper and drizzled with 1 tablespoon (15 ml) balsamic vinegar (optional)

- Soft Medjool dates, pitted and stuffed with pecans or nut/seed butter

- Red bell pepper, halved with seeds removed, with each half filled with some Sun–Dried Tomato Spread (page 142) and stuffed with diced cucumbers and zucchini—all topped with Crème Fraiche (page 140), salt, and pepper.

- Celery stalks filled with your favorite nut/seed butter and topped with cacao nibs and goji berries

- Large celery stalks filled with Chipotle Not Chicken (page 124)

- A hollowed–out cucumber filled with Cilantro Pesto (page 143) or your favorite spread and topped with diced tomatoes

- Sliced apples dipped in Salted Caramel Sauce (page 161)

- A combination of 2 tablespoons (30 g) tahini and 1 tablespoon (20 g) each of honey, cacao nibs, and coconut oil, and a dash of vanilla and sea salt in a bowl placed in the freezer for a few minutes (better than cookie dough!)

- Frozen durian from an Asian market, slightly thawed. Run through a food processor or blender. (see Banana–Berry Soft Serve on page 154 for instructions)

CHEF TIP: You might want to eat this last one when no one is around as it has a strong sulfuric odor, which everyone will assume is coming from you!

Glossary

agave nectar:
A sweet syrup that comes from the agave plant, the same plant that brings us tequila. There is some speculation about how raw it really is, so I suggest using it sparingly. Use clear agave over the brown varieties, which are most likely heated at high temperatures.

arame:
A dark, thin, noodlelike seaweed. Soak for five minutes and rinse before using.

bee pollen:
Considered to be a superfood among athletes. A very good source of complete protein—high in B vitamins, phytonutrients, and enzymes.

blue–green algae:
A type of microalgae that contains an array of vitamins, minerals, enzymes, phytonutrients, and amino acids and is high in chlorophyll. A popular superfood used in smoothies and salads.

Bragg Apple Cider Vinegar:
A raw vinegar that works great in dressings and sauces and can be taken with water as a digestive aid.

buckwheat:
A gluten–free seed used for raw granolas and cereals and a great source of protein. Buckwheat sprouts should be eaten only in moderation, because they can cause sun sensitivity called fagopyrism.

cacao butter:
Fat that has been separated from the cacao bean. Used for chocolate and other desserts.

cacao powder:
Ground cacao beans, also known as cocoa powder. Most supermarkets carry only heated cacao, so find a reputable raw brand at health food stores or online. It is the best plant source of magnesium and a great source of amino acids, especially tryptophan, which helps create serotonin and also contains the stimulating alkaloid theobromine. No wonder chocolate makes us feel so happy.

camu camu:
A superfood from South America made from the berries of the camu camu bush. Considered to have the highest vitamin C content of any plant.

Celtic salt:
A moist, sun–dried sea salt that contains an array of trace minerals.

chia seeds:
An ancient food of the Aztecs, this gluten–free seed is high in essential fatty acids, complete protein, and fiber.

coconut nectar:
A low–glycemic liquid sugar made from the sap of coconut trees.

dulse:
A mild–tasting seaweed that you can buy as little flakes or as larger strips. No soaking is necessary, and it can be eaten straight out of the bag. I like storing the flakes in a sugar dispenser to make it easy to sprinkle on salads.

evaporated cane juice:
Also known as rapadura, this is the least processed form of cane sugar.

galangal:
A root similar to ginger but less spicy and more earthy. Used in various Asian cuisines.

goji berries:
A rich red–orange berry high in antioxidants that has been used for centuries in Chinese medicine as a powerful tonic herb.

Himalayan pink salt:
A prized, high–mineral salt excavated from the Himalayan mountains.

Irish moss:
A seaweed that has been used by herbalists for centuries as an expectorant and digestive aid, but has now become invaluable for its use in desserts and sauces as a substitute for gelatin. It must be rinsed very well and then soaked for twelve hours before use.

jicama:
A sweet and crunchy root vegetable from Mexico similar to a potato; it can be enjoyed raw.

kamut:
An ancient grain high in protein and minerals that is easier to digest for people with wheat sensitivities.

kelp granules:
A great salt substitute, or useful if you want to give something a fishy taste, such as a Thai sauce or "tuna" salad.

kelp noodles:
A sea vegetable product that resembles glass noodles. They take on the flavor of whatever sauce you use them with. Rinse well before using.

lecithin:
A powder usually made from soy that is useful as an emulsifier and thickener in recipes. Look for non–GMO brands.

maca:
A Peruvian root that is dried and ground into a flour. Known as an adaptogenic superfood, it helps support the hormonal, nervous, and cardiovascular systems.

Medjool date:
A soft and chewy date that has a lovely caramel–type flavor and a higher water content than other varieties.

miso:
A fermented Asian condiment usually made from soybeans and rice. I use chickpea miso from Miso Master because it is soy free and has a very nice, mild flavor.

nama shoyu:
A fermented and unpasteurized soy sauce.

nori:
These are the most popular of seaweeds and are used for making sushi rolls. All nori sheets are toasted unless marked otherwise.

nutritional yeast:
A food supplement that is high in B vitamins. It gives raw food dishes a cheesy flavor, similar to that of Parmesan cheese.

palm sugar:
An unrefined, granulated sweetener made from the sap of coconut trees. Has a brown sugar–like flavor, is high in minerals, and can be used in place of evaporated cane juice.

psyllium husk powder:
A fiber–rich dietary supplement that is also used as a thickener in recipes.

rejuvelac:
A fermented beverage made from wheat and rye berries.

rye berries:
A low–gluten cereal grain that can be sprouted or used in essene breads. Can be used to make rejuvelac.

sacha inchi:
Also known as the Inca peanut, this Peruvian seed has the highest natural source of omega–3.

seaweeds:
High in minerals and a great source of iodine, which is essential for the thyroid; they are a great addition to salads and soups.

spirulina:
An ancient single–celled, blue–green algae high in protein, vitamins, minerals, enzymes, phytonutrients, and chlorophyll.

stevia:
The leaves of the stevia plant have been used as a sweetener for centuries. It is extremely sweet with a bitter licorice aftertaste. An acquired taste but favorable for those who are avoiding sugar. Also available in a liquid or powdered form. I use liquid stevia for the recipes in this book.

superfoods:
Foods that have a very high ORAC value (oxygen radical absorbance capacity value—the method to measure antioxidant content) as well as other qualities that are extraordinary. They're considered to be more like whole food supplements. Some are very delicious, such as cacao and goji berries.

tahini:
A delicious paste made of ground sesame seeds. A good source of calcium.

tamari:
A fermented and gluten–free soy sauce appropriate for people with wheat allergies.

tamarind:
An exotic sweet and sour fruit from Asia often used in salad dressings and sauces. Look for it as a seedless paste in Asian food markets.

wakame:
A hearty green seaweed. Soak it in water and then rinse before using.

wheat berries:
Hulled wheat kernel used to make rejuvelac. Can be sprouted and used in essene breads.

wild jungle peanuts:
An ancient heirloom nut from the Amazon. They do not contain aflatoxin, a toxin made by a mold found in American peanuts.

xylitol:
A low–glycemic sweetener usually made from birch trees and corn. It looks and tastes very much like white sugar but without the blood–spiking qualities. It also has antibacterial properties and can help prevent tooth decay and oral candida infections as well as Staphylococcus bacteria when sprayed medicinally in the ears and sinuses. It is a safe alternative sweetener for diabetics, cancer patients, or anyone following a low–sugar diet.

yacon syrup:
A sweet, almost molasseslike syrup that comes from the yacon root.

Zante currants:
A small, sweet variety of black grape. Dried, they are a mini version of a common raisin.

Resources

➤ INGREDIENTS AND EQUIPMENT

- Raw Judita, www.rawjudita.com
- Renegade Health, www.renegadehealth.com
- The Raw Food World, www.therawfoodworld.com
- Raw Guru, www.rawguru.com
- Vita–Mix Blenders, www.vita–mix.com

➤ RAW NEWS, LIFESTYLE, AND COMMUNITY

- Cleanse America, www.cleanseamerica.com
- Raw Food Rehab, www.rawfoodrehab.com
- Renegade Health, www.renegadehealth.com
- Vibrant Living with Dr. Ritamarie, www.drritamarie.com
- Natural News, www.naturalnews.com

➤ RAW FOOD AND HEALTH BLOGS

- Raw Judita, www.rawjudita.com
- Raw on $10 a Day, www.rawon10.blogspot.com
- Raw Foods on a Budget, www.rawfoodsonabudget.com

- Rawmazing, www.rawmazing.com
- Choosing Raw, www.choosingraw.com
- Kristen's Raw, www.kristensraw.com
- Pure Mamas, puremamas.squarespace.com
- Rawdorable, rawdorable.blogspot.com
- Philip McCluskey, www.philipmccluskey.com
- Frederic Patenaude, www.fredericpatenaude.com

➤ RAW FOOD SCHOOLS

- Living Light Culinary Institute, www.rawfoodchcf.com
- Matthew Kenny Academy, www.matthewkenneycuisine.com

➤ BECOME A CERTIFIED HEALTH COACH

- Institute for Integrative Nutrition, www.integrativenutrition.com Tell them I sent you or e–mail me for more info at rawjudita@yahoo.com.

Acknowledgments

Thank you so much to everyone at Quarry Books for believing in me and getting behind this project.

Hugs and kisses to my husband, Matt, who helped bring the vision I had for this book to life through his images.

Much gratitude to my food stylist, Peilin Chen Breller, for bringing her artistry to my recipes.

Many thanks to my recipe testers who helped perfect these recipes and provide invaluable feedback. Major love to my supertesters, Anita Repp, Andrea Lyn, and Raw Rebecca you are my rawkstars!

Thank you Stormy Monday Goods for supplying cutting boards and kitchen utensils.

About the Author

Judita Wignall, author of *Going Raw*, is a certified holistic health counselor from the Institute for Integrative Nutrition and a raw food chef and nutrition educator from the Living Light Culinary Institute. Before becoming passionate about holistic health, she was a commercial actress, model, and musician. She gives lectures, teaches classes, and counsels clients around the country to help them become slimmer, more energetic, radiant, and vibrant. She loves helping people reach their health goals in a way that is doable and delicious. www.rawjudita.com.

Index

A

acai berries, 35

acne. *See* skin.

agave nectar, 32

aging, 10

air toxicity, 13, 21

alcohol, 11

Almond Milk, 15, 47, 48, 50, 53, 68, 78, 128, 153, 156, 157

aloe vera, 35

anger, 21

antibiotics, 22

appetizers. *See* soups, sides & starters.

apples
- Apple Pie Smoothie, 50
- Carrot–Apple Cupcakes, 150
- Cultured Beet–Apple Salad, 139, 140
- Easy Apple Pie with Salted Caramel Sauce, 161, 165
- Fresh Fennel Juice, 70
- Green Day Juice, 70
- Maroon 5 Juice, 70
- Orange–Cranberry–Apple Relish, 140
- Red Delish Lemonade, 70
- Winterland Salad, 103

apricots
- Cherry–Hemp Muesli, 44, 50, 165
- Fruity Kefir, 64, 68, 136
- Stone Fruit Salad with Sweet Almond Ricotta, 40, 141

Astragalus Root Tea, 71

avocados
- Avocado Sauce, 112
- Calexico Salad, 96
- Cherry Bomb Cupcakes, 151
- Chipotle Not–Chicken Salad Wraps, 16, 124, 165
- Creamy Kale Salad with Capers and Hazelnuts, 18, 100
- Garden Smoothie, 53
- Ginger Miso Hand Rolls, 128
- Mango Salsa, 142
- Marinated Mushrooms, 112
- Morning Scramble, 43
- Smoky Guacamole, 36, 86, 165
- Southwest Corn Chowder, 36, 73

B

bananas
- Banana–Berry Soft Serve, 154
- Banana Walnut Oatmeal, 47
- Happy Monkey, 53
- Hazelnut Fig Shake, 57
- Tropico Gelato, 54

barefoot walking, 21

Basic Nut Milk, 56, 59

Basic Water Kefir, 64, 68, 134, 136

bee pollen, 35

beets
- Cultured Beet–Apple Salad, 139, 140
- Ginger Miso Hand Rolls, 128
- Maroon 5 Juice, 70
- Root Vegetable Slaw, 111

bell peppers
- Five–Pepper Vegetable Chili, 36, 123, 140
- Garden Smoothie, 53
- Healthy Mary, 60
- Hot Sauce, 142
- King Crimson Juice, 70
- Nacho Cheese Dip, 36, 37, 86, 127
- Pasta Marinara, 36, 120
- Red Bell Pepper Hummus, 36, 37, 85
- snack ideas, 165
- Thai Veggie Noodles, 116
- Veggies on the Rocks, 68
- Vietnamese Salad Rolls, 131
- Zucchini Noodles Two Ways, 120

benefits, 9–10

beverages. *See also* fermented foods and beverages.
- Cocojito, 29, 63
- Fresh Fennel Juice, 70
- Grape Chia Fresca, 68
- Green Day Juice, 70
- Green Juice Mocktail, 68
- Healthy Mary, 60
- Indian–Spiced Orange, 68
- juice fasting, 15
- juicers, 27
- King Crimson Juice, 70
- Lemon–Lime Chia Fresca, 68
- Maroon 5 Juice, 70
- Milk and Honey Refresher, 68
- Red Delish Lemonade, 70
- Sparkling Grapefruit, 68
- Strawberry Daiquiri, 64
- Succo di Pomodoro, 70
- teas, 71
- Vanilla Cashew Hemp Milk, 18, 37, 59
- Veggies on the Rocks, 68
- Watermelon–Fennel–Mint Chiller, 67

blenders, 27

blending tips, 30

blueberries
- Banana–Berry Soft Serve, 154
- Wild Blueberry–Meyer Lemon Cheesecake Squares, 162

Body Ecology Diet, The (Donna Gates), 22, 23

Boutenko, Victoria, 12, 53

breakfast
- Banana Walnut Oatmeal, 47
- Cardamom Raisin Chia Pudding, 48
- Cherry–Hemp Muesli, 44, 50, 165
- Cultured Beet–Apple Salad, 139, 140
- Hazelnut Chocolate Chia Pudding, 49
- Morning Scramble, 43
- Stone Fruit Salad with Sweet Almond Ricotta, 40, 141
- Superfood Chia Pudding, 48

broccoli
- cruciferous family, 89
- Lemony Garlic Broccoli Bowl, 127

burdock root, 14

Butternut Squash Noodles with Sage Cream, 119

cabbage
- Colorful Cabbage Salad, 36, 99
- Creamy Kale Salad with Capers and Hazelnuts, 18, 100
- Cultured Beet–Apple Salad, 139, 140
- Jalapeño Kraut, 139
- Marinated Mushrooms, 112
- Quick Pickled Cabbage, 112
- Vietnamese Salad Rolls, 131

C

cacao beans, 34

Café Gratitude, 57

calcium, 10

Calexico Salad, 96

camu camu berries, 35

cancer, 23

candida, 19, 22, 23

cantaloupe
- Green Juice Mocktail, 68
- Orange Bee Love, 56

carcinogens, 11

Cardamom Raisin Chia Pudding, 48

carrots
- Carrot–Apple Cupcakes, 150
- Carrot–Ginger Coconut Smoothies, 16
- Carrot–Ginger Coconut Soup, 29, 77
- Colorful Cabbage Salad, 36, 99
- Curried Carrots, 94
- Five–Pepper Vegetable Chili, 36, 123, 140
- Ginger Miso Hand Rolls, 128
- Jalapeño Kraut, 139
- King Crimson Juice, 70
- Lemony Garlic Broccoli Bowl, 127
- Root Vegetable Slaw, 111
- shredded, 37
- Thai Veggie Noodles, 116
- Vietnamese Salad Rolls, 131

Cashew Hemp Milk, 18, 59

Cashew Milk, 15, 47, 48, 50, 53, 68, 78, 128, 153, 156

cauliflower
- Cauliflower Couscous, 90
- Cauliflower Smash, 93
- Curried Cauliflower Soup, 81